"Memories straight from a mother's heart. Her vivid memoirs will trigger your own remembrances of parenting small children. If your children are still under foot, you'll discover a cherished friend as you see yourself on the pages of *Muddy Feet On the Narrow Path*. Told with nostalgia and love that demonstrates God's willingness to help mothers of all ages."

Marion Bond West
Author, Contributing Editor
Guideposts

"There are many days that I feel alone and incompetent as a mother. *Muddy Feet On the Narrow Path* is a candid and heartfelt reminder of how God is in the midst of each day, holding our hands and guiding us through the trials, tears, and triumphs of being a mother. Every day is a new experience and a new lesson to be learned."

Donna Labonte
Wife of racecar driver Bobby Labonte

Muddy Feet on the Narrow Path

God bless you on the narrow Path!

Donna Tobin Smith

Matthew 7:13-14

Muddy Feet on the Narrow Path

Encouragement for staying focused on God, even in the
messy times of our lives.

Donna Tobin Smith

TATE PUBLISHING & *Enterprises*

Published by Tate Publishing & Enterprises, LLC
127 E. Trade Center Terrace | Mustang, Oklahoma 73064 USA
1.888.361.9473 | www.tatepublishing.com

Tate Publishing is committed to excellence in the publishing industry. The company reflects the philosophy established by the founders, based on Psalm 68:11,
"The Lord gave the word and great was the company of those who published it."

Book design copyright © 2008 by Tate Publishing, LLC. All rights reserved.
Cover design by Jonathan Lindsey
Interior design by Janae J. Glass

Published in the United States of America

ISBN: 978-1-60604-234-2
1. Christian Living: Relationships: Family
2. Inspiration: Motivational: General Religious Inspiration
08.06.17

To my beloved husband, David, who leads our precious family on the narrow path, and to God's greatest gifts in our lives, Joshua, Daniel, and Benjamin.

Acknowledgments

First and foremost, to God be the glory. I would have no stories of hope and faith to share if it weren't for my Heavenly Father. I thank Him for enfolding our family in His care and for His faithfulness to His promises.

I would also like to thank my father and mother, Bob and Shirley Tobin, for their love and encouragement and for teaching me about the Lord as a little girl. Thanks also to Sheila, Keith, and Kemp for being my companions on the narrow path as a child, and a special thank-you to their families for their love and support.

My deepest gratitude also to my father and mother-in-law, Richard and Jane Smith, the kindest people I know, and the whole Smith family. What a blessing it has been to be part of your family.

Thank you over and over to Reverend Ben Shepherd, my pastor and friend, and his wife, Alice, the one who keeps me singing.

To Doris Stokes and Lynn Myers, thanks for being good listeners and faithful friends.

To Chad Killebrew, my first editor, and the finest newspaper man I know. Thank you and your staff at *The Dispatch* for your support and encouragement through our many years together.

Thanks also to my dear friends and supporters in my Sunday school class, The Father's Faithful, at Bethel United Methodist Church. You have lived up to your name in every way. Thank you for being my most "captive" audience!

A special thanks to all of you who faithfully read my column in the newspaper and have encouraged me along the way. You know who you are!

To my editor, Kylie, Mrs. Martha Power, and all those who helped to put my stories in print. Thank you for helping me fulfill my calling to share my lessons in faith with people I may never meet.

To Marion Bond West and Donna Labonte, thank you both for your encouraging words and your prayers. God bless your families.

And to you, my mighty men: David, Josh, Daniel, and Ben. You are my greatest blessings, my greatest joy, my inspiration. I could never find the words to say how much I love you.

Table of Contents

Introduction

It was 1996. Our boys were thirteen, eleven, and nine years old. We had just come home from the beach when my husband picked up the stack of newspapers that had accumulated while we were gone. Before long, he was calling me to "Come look." He had found the perfect job for me. Our hometown newspaper was looking for a columnist, a religion columnist, to be exact.

If by some miracle I could convince the editors to let me write that column, I knew that it would never be a job for me. It would be my privilege and my honor to share the lessons that God was teaching me as a wife and mother. As sure as a minister or a missionary is called to serve, I knew that God had a specific call for my life and had believed for a long time that He wanted me to leave a written legacy of life lessons, not only for my family, but for other families as well.

The newspaper took a chance on me. Through the years I have listened and recorded my family's life story. But the interesting thing is that as I've recorded our story, I've recorded your family's story too. Over and over you have told me that you understood. In the good times and the bad times, the crazy hectic moments and the peaceful calm, you let me know that you have felt what I felt. You have been on the same journeys, and like my family, the Lord has carried your family in the midst of joy and heartache.

Yes, these are my stories, but they're your stories too. The Lord has allowed me to be His instrument to record our desires for our families, our prayers, and our praise for His faithfulness. As long as I have breath in me and the Lord allows, I will continue to share our stories. Thank you for your prayers and continued support.

Donna Tobin Smith

Are all the children in?

One of the things I am most thankful for in my life is a Godly heritage. My daddy was raised in a time when large families were common. Many times he and his brothers and sisters would play all over the neighborhood well into the evening. But as the day settled into night and the children made their way back home, my grandma was often heard asking, "Daddy, are all the children in?"

Grandma wasn't just concerned with their physical safety. She was even more concerned about their souls. And just as she taught her own children about spiritual truths, she also taught her grandchildren.

Grandma kept the cousins whose parents worked. My mother stayed at home with us, but once in a while on a special day, I would get to spend the day with Grandma. Every afternoon at the same time Grandma would again ask if all the children were in. This time it was for Bible reading and prayer time.

As Grandma knelt and called every one of her children and grandchildren by name, I do recall an occasional spit-wad sailing past her head (most of my cousins were boys). But I also remember that Grandma's prayers weren't just shopping lists of requests. They were filled with praise and thanksgiving. She talked to Jesus like He was right there in the room with us, just like an old friend.

Grandma has been gone for many years now, but I'm sure her prayers for me have been answered as I look into the faces of my husband and our three sons.

On a weekend trip to the beach, I went by the hotel office to ask a question.

"Is there a church service on the beach?" I asked. "Or is there an early service at a church nearby?" Checkout was at eleven a.m. The lady at the counter looked at me rather oddly.

"We don't get many questions like that," she replied. "I have no idea. But maybe you can check the yellow pages in the phonebook."

I can't say that it was easy to get three boys, ages eight, eleven, and thirteen, to put on Sunday clothes at Myrtle Beach to be at church at 8:30. But as we listened to 1 Corinthians 13, the beautiful love chapter being read, and sang "Great is Thy Faithfulness," I knew the hassle to get there was well worth the effort.

That night, as we settled back into our own beds and I picked up the Bible to read, I heard one of the boys ask,

"Do we have to read the Bible? We've already been to church today." For a moment my mind's eye caught a glimpse of a spitwad whizzing by Grandma's head. Then I thought of two of those boy cousins who were in that room every afternoon with Grandma. They're Baptist preachers now. I smile.

People say that was a simpler time. Maybe so. But it seems to me that amidst the schedules, appointments, meetings, and deadlines, there is a question that still needs to be answered, and it has more to do with the soul than physical safety.

Are all the children in?

The worth of a child

It happens all the time. I'm driving down the road, lost in my own thoughts, when my peaceful silence is interrupted by a voice from the back of the van.

"I wish Papaw was Bob Tobinlake."

Before I know it, I am involved in a conversation with my youngest son that makes no sense to me whatsoever.

"Papaw is Bob Tobin," I say.

"What do you mean by Tobinlake?"

"I wish Papaw was Bob Tobinlake," he repeated.

"Then I could be an action figure."

I scratched my head and looked at him in my rearview mirror.

"What in the world are you talking about?" I asked.

"Well," he explained, "if Papaw was Bob Tobinlake, like Bob Timberlake, then maybe he would have an action figure made of me."

He had obviously heard of the dolls that were made of each of Bob Timberlake's grandchildren. Mr. Timberlake is a well-known artist who lives in our town. I guess he figured that being an action figure was the next best thing.

The conversation ended there. He didn't say anything else about it, but I couldn't help but wonder where the thought came from. Maybe it's because every time we go by the Timberlake Gallery I say, "Someday I'm going to find the time to stop in there." Maybe it's because our whole family is artistic and we love to draw.

No, it wasn't so much the art, although we all enjoy it. It was more than that. My son was telling me that he wanted to be somebody. He wanted to be recognized. He wanted to be special.

I guess that's pretty hard when you have two big brothers. You're not the biggest, you're not the tallest, you're not the strongest. You can't stay up as long. The list goes on and on.

I try to be a good parent, but as I look at my growing children, I realize that by the time I figure out how to do it right, they'll be grown and gone. And so I struggle. And I pray that God will show me what to do and how to do it when it comes to parenting my children.

The children in my home aren't the only ones who crave to find their worth in this world. As a teacher, I am faced every day with children who feel worthless. Yes, my job is to teach them to be better readers, but it is also to lead them to find value and talents within themselves.

When my oldest son was small, I always asked him how much he was worth. And with my prodding, he always answered, "A million bucks." (When I asked him how much Daddy was worth, he always said, "A plug nickel." I wonder where he got that?!)

As I attempt daily to demonstrate to each of my children how valuable they are, I can think of no better example for me than Jesus. Throughout His life, Jesus was surrounded by people who were of little importance or influence, as far as the society of His day was concerned. From the lowly shepherds at His birth to Simon, the leper, and Zacchaeus, the tax collector, Jesus served and blessed those who were often unnoticed by others. With love and compassion, He gave worth to the worthless and hope to the hopeless.

And He's still doing it today. He is still saying to us, as He did to His disciples, "Let the little children come to me, and do not hinder them, for the kingdom of heaven belongs to such as these" (Matthew 19:14).

But it's not only the children who have value to Him. He's pointing to the single mothers and fathers, the stay-at-home parents, the overworked and the weary too. The world may look at outward appearances and possessions, but Jesus looks past the fancy clothes and cars, past the big offices and important titles, right to the heart. That's who we really are anyway.

It would be wonderful if my boys' papaw was a famous artist. But it's not so bad that he's a plain old papaw who goes to church every Sunday and tries to live a godly life. In fact, it just doesn't get much better than that.

Church is about more than just getting

Excuses, excuses. I was so tired of hearing excuses. The young people of the church had been working on a musical program for weeks. I was helping paint the scenery, so I had seen most of the practices. I had insisted that all three of my boys take part in the program. To hear them talk, you would have thought they had been sentenced to hard labor and torture.

We have a fifteen-minute drive to church, and during those weeks of practice one thing never failed: Every Wednesday night at least one boy had a stomachache, or a sore throat, or an earache, or a toothache, or a backache. It was too rainy or too sunny. They were too tired or had too much homework. The songs were too babyish. There were too many words to learn and the practices were too long. And so it went, week after week.

Then came the straw that broke the camel's back. I had endured the excuses and complaints pretty well until that Wednesday night when one of the boys started his usual grumbling. It was pretty much a one-way conversation, him griping and me looking at him in my rearview mirror.

"Mom," he started, "I don't see why you're making us be in this dumb program. I know why you make me go to Sunday school. I even understand why you make me go to preaching. I don't always like it, but I know it's good for me. But I don't understand why you're making me be in this program. Mom, I don't get one thing out of this Wednesday night practice."

It was all I could do to hold the van on the road. I could feel my mama finger rising to the rearview mirror. That's the finger that wags at the child when the mama wants to make a point that should never be forgotten. I took a deep breath before I spoke.

"In that case," I replied, "just consider it your gift. Who taught you that you were supposed to be on the receiving end of everything you do? Since when do you have to get something every time you walk through the church doors? The sermon that doesn't mean anything to you may change another person's life forever. A song that you don't like may be a blessing to someone else. There are people who are looking forward to this program. Your witness can make a tremendous impact on people's lives for Jesus. It should be your gift to God and the people."

We continued on to church, but it was a different ride than I had grown accustomed to on Wednesday nights. There was a welcomed silence as we all reflected on the conversation that had just taken place.

I guess I could have shrugged off their complaints and excuses with, "Boys will be boys," or, "You know how children are." Evidently, parents have done that in the past because many grownups today are using the very same excuses that my boys used. They can't come to church because Sunday is the only day the whole family can be together.

They can't bring the children to Sunday school because it is the only day they can sleep late. They don't get anything out of church, anyway, so why should they come?

The program was a wonderful witness for Jesus. Months later people were still talking about how blessed they were by it.

As for my boys, the best reward for all their hard work was not what they got out of it. The real reward will be the men they become as they continue to learn about the importance of giving.

Let the Good Shepherd bring you home if you're lost

"Are you lost?" I looked at the wandering young man with questioning eyes. From my morning duty post at the middle school where I teach, I am getting really good at picking out the kids who are roaming the halls, choosing to be in the wrong place at the wrong time. With a snort, the boy turned back in the direction of his homeroom and trudged to his class.

Was he really lost? No. He knew where he was supposed to be. He had made a conscious choice to be somewhere else. I knew that. And by the looks of things from my morning duty perspective, he's not the only one making the choice to get "lost" on the way to class in the mornings.

It is a common concern among the teachers at my school. Of course, it is usually the same students over and over who get lost, just a handful who make life hard for those of us who are responsible for them every minute of every school day. The truth is, they seem to enjoy being lost. Until they are caught and suffer major consequences, some of them put a lot of effort into not being found.

Not me. I've been lost once or twice myself. But I can't ever remember getting lost on purpose. Call me directionally challenged. Maybe I just don't pay attention. Whatever the reason, I know one thing: I don't like being lost. I don't like the warm flush that begins at the base of my neck and rises until my face glows with panic. I don't like not being where I am supposed to be.

I remember the days when my own children were young. It was hard to keep three preschool boys under tow. Because I had only two hands, there was always one boy on the loose. The boy who was free from my grip was never concerned with the fact that he could get lost when we went to the grocery store or the mall. It was always me, guarding and protecting, making sure he didn't stray. In his mind, as long as he knew where he was, why should it matter so much to his mommy?

But there were times when the boys were lost and they knew it. For years they have recounted a harrowing experience of being lost in the woods. They can all laugh about it now, but at the time it was very scary. The details are a little sketchy, and I still don't know everything that happened. I wasn't there. But from their accounts, they were visiting their older cousin. I think he was about eleven at the time. They remember a rope. Somehow the rope was left in the woods and they needed it. Thinking they would retrieve the rope quickly, they all traipsed back into the woods to get it, but somehow they got turned around.

Hours passed and they knew that the sun would be going down soon. That's when the panic set in, according to the boys. They had followed their cousin around and around like little ducks in a row. After all, these were his woods. A right turn would have put them in his backyard, where they had started. But a wrong turn would put them near a busy road. They heard the whir of the cars as they passed and knew that they were close to the edge of the woods. But their cousin thought he would be in trouble if he came out of the woods any place except his yard, so he wouldn't even consider leaving the woods any other way.

In my oldest son's version, he saved the day. He was the one who saw light and insisted that his brothers rise up in mutiny against their cousin and follow him until they reached the light. In my middle son's rendition, he spotted a telephone pole and, screaming and crying, broke away from the group and headed for safety. My youngest son was too little to remember anything except that he began to cry, and when they finally emerged from the dark, scary woods, his uncle, who had been driving his car up and down the road searching for them, saved them from being lost forever. Their cousin blamed the rope for the whole mess.

Perhaps you have your own version of a similar story. Maybe you've been physically lost yourself. Maybe someone you love has strayed off the narrow path and found themselves lost in doubt or rebellion, unable to admit even to themselves how lost they really are.

If that's the case, remember the uncle in the story. Even when the boys didn't know it, he was searching for them. Like the Good Shepherd in the Bible, he was searching for the one who wouldn't admit he was lost and for the one who followed the others and couldn't find his own way. He was searching for the one who was frightened and the one who didn't know where to turn. He searched until he found them and took them safely home.

Are you lost too? Someone is searching for you. Are you ready to be found? There is safety in the arms of the Good Shepherd. Why don't you let Him carry you home today?

Yes, it's okay for Christians to say no

We were at a chicken pie supper at church when I caught the end of a conversation that my sister-in-law was having with some people at our table.

"We're going to go home tonight and practice," I heard her say. She put her arm around my brother's shoulders before she continued. "Okay," she said. "Let's start now. Repeat after me. *No*," she said, drawing out the word. "Come on, you try it."

"*Nnnn*," he started. "Sorry, I can't do it," he mumbled.

"That's why we're practicing," she replied. "One more time. It's such a short, simple little word."

"*Nnnn*," he tried again.

"I know," she suggested. "Let's do it this way. I'll give you a situation and you just say the word. Let's say that someone comes up to you and says, 'I have an outbuilding that I'd like for you to paint.' Now, what do you say?"

"Nine hundred dollars," my brother replied.

"It's going to be a long night," my sister-in-law said and sighed.

My brother is a painter. In addition to his regular forty-hour-a-week job, he puts in a lot of extra hours on the side. Not only does he paint, but he does all sorts of jobs that people would rather not do themselves. That day, my sister-in-law had helped him pressure wash a house, and they were both bone-tired. But he still had a long list of jobs and people asking him to do even more work every day. That's why they were practicing.

"Why can't you just say no?" she had asked.

It's a question that I've been asking myself lately too, especially on nights when I am too bone-tired to sleep. Why can't I just say no?

I don't know. Maybe I really don't want to. Most of the time I just say yes and then whine when I get so stressed and overwhelmed that I can hardly go.

"Guess who they asked to speak at the banquet next week?" I asked my husband the other day.

"Who?" he asked.

"Me," I replied with the most frazzled look I could muster.

"Oh stop," he said. "You know you love talking in front of an audience. So don't give me that 'I can't believe I said yes' look. You did say yes, didn't you?"

Did he really even need to ask?

I used to hear a certain song on the radio and imagine my

boys singing it about me someday. It was a song about a mama burning the midnight oil down on her knees in prayer.

What a beautiful legacy, I thought. How wonderful it would be if my boys would someday conjure up an image like that of me. Yes, I've spent many nights burning the midnight oil, but the image they would much more likely conjure up is one of a Mama making lunches, helping with homework, making costumes for school plays, or running out at midnight to buy supplies for a last-minute project. And my prayers at the midnight hour are usually a panicked plea for the Lord to give me strength as I struggle to finish my tasks before I collapse into bed.

The Bible speaks of a busy man in the eighteenth chapter of Exodus. The Bible says that Moses "took his seat to serve as judge for the people, and they stood around him from morning till evening" (Exodus 18:13).

> When Moses' father-in-law, Jethro, saw what was happening, he said to Moses, "You and these people will only wear yourselves out. The work is too heavy for you, you cannot handle it alone" (Exodus 18:17–18).

> So he told Moses to find capable men and divide the work, to delegate the simpler cases to others. "If you do this and God so commands, you will be able to stand the strain, and all these people will be satisfied" (Exodus 18:23).

Do you suppose that God could be speaking to my brother and me as He spoke to Moses? Could it really be that we don't have to do it all? Is it possible that those around us would be just as satisfied if we shared the load, if we didn't try to do everything for everyone?

It's hard to say, but I guess it's worth a try. If fact, I think I'll start practicing right now.

"*Nnnn. Nnnn.*"

I guess my sister-in-law was right. It's going to be a long night.

Only the truth will set us free

I remember it like it was yesterday. My curly haired three-year-old and I were having a serious discussion. I had made an appointment to have a portrait made of all three boys that week, but something was wrong.

One look at this boy and I could see that one of his curls was missing, the big one, right at the top of his forehead, cut off all the way to his scalp. I couldn't believe it. I had heard of children giving themselves haircuts, but why now? What kind of portrait would this make?

"What happened to your hair?" I asked, obviously upset. I should have known. It didn't take him long to see that his mommy was not pleased.

"It just blew right off," he answered, searching my face

for my reaction. Before I could reply, he tried again. "That big old dinosaur came in my room and just licked it off."

"The truth," I said, "I want the truth. Tell me what really happened and tell me now." I finally did get the truth. And just as I had suspected, my curious three-year-old had found a pair of scissors and cut his own hair.

As the years have gone by, we have had many discussions with all three boys about how important it is to be truthful. We've told them that no matter what they have done, it's always better to tell the truth. "You'll be in more trouble if you don't," we've reminded them. And yet from time to time we still deal with a boy in our home who has exaggerated, twisted the truth, hidden facts, made up stories, and denied the obvious. Does it matter? How important is it to tell the truth?

When I was a little girl, the word "lie" was a bad word in our family. We could say that he "told a story" or he fibbed. But there was something about the word lie that was so unacceptable that we were not even allowed to utter the word.

And yet, like my boys, I can remember times when I exaggerated, twisted the truth, hid facts, made up stories, and denied the obvious. And like my boys, I knew better. Why is it so hard for us to be truthful? Is it because of fear? Has it become a habit that we can't break?

I remember another time when all three boys were lined up and questioned about an incident at home. Someone had obviously leaned a nail against a tire on his dad's car. Fortunately, Dad saw it before he backed out of the garage. After an ordeal that went on for what seemed like hours, the little one confessed.

The only thing he couldn't come up with was a reason

that made sense. But then, he never would, because the middle one, we found out later, had actually put the nail there so his dad would have a flat tire and not be able to take him to soccer practice. He didn't want to go. And because Dad said, "If nobody confesses, I'm going to punish you all," the little one confessed.

Unfortunately, we live in a world that doesn't make much of a commitment to truth. We have strayed so far from the absolute truths in the Word of God that we are now making up our own truth based on our own opinions.

In John 14:6, Jesus says, "I am the way, and the truth, and the life. No one comes to the Father except through me." We have to know the truth to be committed to it.

We had the picture made anyway. And every time I look at the boy in the picture with the missing curl, I am reminded of God's promise to me and my boys: that through Jesus, we will know the truth, and the truth will set us free.

Making the right turns

It's six o'clock on Monday morning. The alarm goes off. I drag myself out of bed at 6:15, knowing that I'm already running late.

"Can you fix me eggs this morning?" asks my oldest son as I'm drying my hair.

"I'll try," I answer. "I'm hurrying.'"

By 7:10 I'm in the kitchen, separating the yolks from the whites. The big boy eats only egg whites these days. In the meantime, I fix breakfast for the youngest boy.

The middle son just wants to talk. He talks about a movie, a chemistry test, and the administrative board meeting at church that night where he would have to speak as a youth representative.

I check the clock. I can make it.

"Feed the animals. You're going to have to eat your sandwich in the van. What in the world are you doing?" I ask my youngest son. He's stuffing Ziploc bags in his shoes.

"My shoes stink so bad I sprayed them with Lysol, and now they're wet.

"Here, try wax paper," I say. "Stuff that in your shoes."

I put the egg whites on a plate, yell good-bye to the big boys, and grab my things.

Seven twenty-six and all is well. For about thirty seconds, that is. I get all the way to the end of the driveway when I remember my medicine. I put the van in reverse.

"But Mama," my son shouted, "the bus!"

"I'll hurry," I promise.

Seven twenty-seven. I have one minute to beat the bus. If I don't get ahead of the bus, my eight-minute trip to school will turn into fifteen minutes and I'll be late for sure. I'm getting ready to pull out of the driveway when I see it: a log truck, going my way, of course. I pull out behind it and hold my breath as we get to the turn where it's either me or the bus.

"No, no, no! " I shout as the log truck waits for the bus to turn in front of it. Now I'm behind the truck and the bus.

The log truck turns off. I'm still behind the bus, but I do have another choice. There is a road that runs parallel to the road I usually take to school. It's a little longer and I'd be taking a chance, but I decide to go for it, only to see a transfer truck turn ahead of me onto the little country road.

I feel tears welling up in my eyes. All I want is to be at work on time. I follow it almost all the way to the road I usually take and see not one, but two buses pulling out.

One is the same bus that turned in front of the log truck near my house.

As we near the school, the first bus stops to let a line of cars turn in front of it. I start laughing hysterically.

"Stop it, Mama. You're scaring me," said my son.

.   .   .   .   .

"Good morning." I nod to the secretary and the principal as I try to catch my breath.

Seven forty-five. Right on time. I sign in.

Let me guess. You've been there too. You try to make the right turns and a log truck pulls out in front of you. Like Moses in the wilderness, sometimes no matter how hard we try, the road is blocked.

We know where we want to be. We feel the call of God in our lives. So we stumble and stop. We change directions and try again. And ultimately, if we let Him, God leads us exactly where He wants us to be, in His perfect time, not ours.

I don't mind the work when I get there. I know my calling. But I don't always like the journey. Too many unexpected stops. Too many detours. So hold my hand, Lord. Don't ever let me go. Because with You directing every turn I make, I'll be exactly where You want me to be. Right on time.

Loving enough to be tough

"What are you doing in my kitchen?" I had been walking on the treadmill in the basement, oblivious to what was going on upstairs. He looked up at me with his big brown eyes then quickly ducked his head. He was in trouble. He wasn't allowed in my kitchen, and he knew it.

My youngest son probably had something to do with this. Sure enough, I looked up and there he stood.

"What is he doing in my kitchen?"

"Well, Mama, he was on the front porch and he looked lonely and hungry. The garage doors were closed, so he couldn't get to his food, so I decided to let him come through the house."

"You didn't let him walk across the carpet in the den?" I asked.

"No, I carried him."

Now we were getting somewhere. So this is how Doby the dog had gotten into the house.

"Tell me," I said to my son, "if you were carrying him through to the garage, why is he sitting in my kitchen, acting like he belongs here?"

I know what you're thinking. What's the big deal? A dog in the kitchen. Lots of people have dogs in their kitchens, even sleeping in their beds, for that matter. But not Doby. Doby is an outside dog, always has been and always will be. My husband and I decided a long time ago that raising three boys in our house was chaos enough. We certainly didn't need an inside dog to add to the activity.

We love Doby. He's a good dog. He's nice to our cats. He chases squirrels and barks at the crows who take more than their share of the pecans in our yard. So it's certainly not that we don't care about Doby. But we do have rules. And we expect those rules to be followed.

I asked again, "If you were carrying him through to the garage, why is he sitting in the kitchen?"

"Well, Mama, he wanted to stop for a minute. So I let him down and now he won't budge."

"What do you mean, 'he won't budge'?" The door to the garage was two feet from where Doby was sitting. I looked over at my son. "Did you think of this?" I grabbed Doby by the collar, dragged him to the door, and out he went.

"Oh, Mama," said my son, "I couldn't have done that. I love him too much."

I wheeled around to face my son.

"How many times," I asked, "have I dragged you by your

collar? How many times have I *made* you do something you didn't want to do because it was right? Do you think that just because I make you do something that I don't love you? I make you do the right thing *because* I love you."

God loved the children of Israel. He promised to deliver them out of the hands of the Egyptians and into the Promised Land. But sometimes they were stubborn. Sometimes, like Doby, they refused to be led.

They were so stiff-necked, in fact, that after returning from the mountain where he received God's laws and instructions for the people, Moses found them singing, dancing, and worshiping a golden calf. So Moses "grabbed them by their collars." He threw down the tablets inscribed with the Word of God, breaking them into pieces. "And He took the calf they had made and burned it in the fire; then He ground it to powder, scattered it on the water and *made* the Israelites drink it" (Exodus 32:20, emphasis mine).

Because He didn't care about them? No. In fact, the next day Moses approached God on their behalf to make atonement for their sins.

So, Doby, watch out for the long arm of the law. I will teach my boy that as your master, he must lead you, even if he has to drag you sometimes. And boys, when you feel that tug on your collars, don't worry. It's only me. The one who loves you.

Don't ever give up, even when words seem to fall on deaf ears

My mother was calling. Her voice was loud and clear, and I knew exactly what she was saying. But if she thought for one minute that I would listen to her, she thought wrong.

I was six years old and out on the swing set in our back-yard having the time of my life. It had begun to rain, gently at first, but quickly turned into a torrential downpour. It was wonderful. I loved every drop. I loved the flowing trail of rain as it drizzled down my face and dripped off my chin. My hair was soppy wet, and my clothes were drenched. I had never had so much fun.

But soon I heard my mother's voice again. She was trying to ruin my fun. I could see her at the back door, hands on her hips, a scowl spreading across her face. Again, she called for me to come inside, emphasizing exactly what would happen to me if I didn't come in that very minute. I remember thinking that she was making a mountain out of a molehill, an expression that I had obviously picked up from her. She had a way of rubbing off on me even when I didn't want her to. But today I wouldn't be persuaded. No amount of begging or pleading or cajoling would change my mind. I would swing until I was tired of swinging. I was having too much fun to stop.

Mama had four babies. I was her oldest. On that day I knew she was tending to the other babies and wouldn't think of bringing them outside to retrieve me, nor leave them inside to come and drag me in. Boy, was I wrong. Not only did she stomp outside to gather up my sopping self in her strong arms, but the flyswatter welts that I wore on my legs the next day were a reminder that when my mother spoke, it was my duty and obligation as her child to listen.

That was a long time ago, but the memory of that day is still vivid in my mind. I wish I could say that I learned my lesson and always listened to my mother from that day on. But there were sassy days of adolescence to follow and defiant teenage years. I honestly don't remember saying anything disrespectful to my mother, although there were many times I thought those sassy words, with the exception of one time when I was about sixteen years old. My father got my full attention, however, before the last sassy word left my mouth, and I knew that for the rest of my days I would never talk back to my mother.

But I still didn't always listen to my mother's advice. Oh,

I pretended to listen. Sometimes I even heard the words, but I quickly gave them permission to go in one ear and out the other. In all my worldly wisdom (or was it my youthful foolishness?), on many occasions I convinced myself that Mama just didn't know what she was talking about. In my foolish young mind she was old-fashioned, and her advice was out-of-date.

What in the world was I thinking? As a mother now, I am the one at the back door with my hands on my hips. Sometimes my words also fall on deaf ears. No matter how clearly I speak, no matter how much I increase the volume, my words go in one ear and out the other. In fact, not only do I see it in my own home but in my classroom and in my church as well. Christian mothers and fathers are shouting out wisdom of many years of studying God's Word, years of experiences that have seen them through times of trouble and heartache, years of praying and depending on God's wisdom and strength daily, and yet often the children do not hear. Instead it is the world that tells them that self-esteem is better than self-respect, that pleasure is better than responsibility, that the morals and values that Christian parents treasure are outdated, reserved only for those with small, closed minds.

I don't mind telling you, it makes me angry. Don't think for one minute I don't know who is behind all this. Every Sunday school lesson I teach, every Bible passage I read, every prayer I pray, the devil hits me a little harder. And he hits me where it hurts the most. He tries his best to entwine himself into the lives of those I love more than life itself. He deceives and entices.

But, by granny, I will not go down without a fight. I will

not compromise, and I will not give up. He will not silence me, and I will not believe that my words will always fall on deaf ears. No, like the old song says, *I shall not be, I shall not be moved.*

I will cling to God's promises for godly parents and their families. I will keep talking, keep persuading, and convincing. And in the weak times when I am weary of the fight, I will not give up because I know that "greater is He that is in (me) than He that is in the world" (1 John 4:4, KJV).

Facing the consequences is never easy

He was clearly upset.

What was supposed to be the most fun day of the whole school year had ended on a sour note. The boy had planned to go home with a friend after school. He had tried to remember everything he would need: toothbrush, socks, and especially his portable compact disc player. His mother knew CD players weren't allowed at school. But she would make an exception this time if he left it in his overnight bag in her room (she taught at his school).

It was a perfect day for field day. The end-of-grade tests were over, and it was a day to relax and enjoy.

The details are sketchy at this point, but somehow the CD player with headphones got out of the overnight bag and onto the boy's ears. Soon, the boy was lounging on the bleachers, basking in the sunshine, moving to the rhythm of the music as he watched the events on the field.

But the peacefulness didn't last long. According to the boy, the teacher was more than mad.

"You know the rules!" she yelled. "No CD players at school. Didn't you read the handbook?"

Then she took the CD player.

And so the boy explained the whole unfortunate situation to his mother after school while the friend listened.

"She screamed at me," the boy complained.

"That's right," said his friend. "She sure did."

Of course, he couldn't help but add that maybe she had to scream because the boy's music was so loud in his headphones that he couldn't have heard her if she hadn't. He looked at his mother with pleading eyes.

"Everybody else was doing it," he said. "Mom, there were even people outside with guitars. Does the handbook allow guitars at school? It's all music. What's wrong with listening to a little music?"

The boy was really getting wound up now. He looked at his mother in anticipation.

"Do something," he pleaded. Then he waited for her to speak. When she finally did speak, it was not what he wanted to hear.

"Sorry, buddy," she said. "You don't have a leg to stand on. You have no defense."

The boy couldn't believe his ears.

"Just because everybody else is doing it certainly doesn't make it right," his mother said. "The fact is, your teacher chose to enforce the rules of the school. Others didn't. You're right about that. No, it doesn't seem fair, and yes, there are lots of things worse than listening to a CD player at field day. But you knew the rules. They're listed right in the handbook, just like your teacher said."

There are lots of other rules in the handbook the students are completely unaware of, they say. Never mind that they signed off that they read and agreed to abide by the rules stated in the handbook at the beginning of the school year, rules that refer to proper dress and appropriate language, for example.

"But everybody else is wearing that," students might say. "Everybody else uses crude language. Therefore, my behavior is excused and acceptable."

I don't think so.

Believe it or not, there are even adults who act this way. Everybody else accepts that lifestyle, so it must be okay. Everybody else goes to those places. Everybody else reads those magazines, watches those programs. So what's the big deal?

Here's the deal. We have a handbook too. It's called the Bible. When we accept Jesus into our hearts, we, in essence, sign off on the handbook. When the Bible says, "Don't follow the ways of the wicked, don't do what evil people do" (Proverbs 4:14), that's what it means. What could we possibly not understand about "do not do anything unless it is right, stay away from evil" (Proverbs 4:27)?

So far, the boy has survived the consequences of his disobedience. But he isn't happy. Suffering consequences is never a pleasant experience. But maybe, just maybe, he'll think before he does something else just because everybody is doing it. And no matter how harmless and insignificant it seems, if the handbook says "don't," maybe next time, he won't.

Lessons learned never cease

We were just leaving church when a friend waved us back.

"Don't forget," she said, "we've rented the skating rink for the children on Wednesday night. We'll have the whole rink to ourselves, so bring somebody with you. Young, old, it doesn't matter, just come!"

My older sons were busy with ball practice, but my youngest son and I decided to go. After all, I needed the exercise, and as wobbly as I am on skates, I still thought that skating might be a good alternative to the treadmill that night.

At four o'clock on Wednesday afternoon, I remembered what my friend had said about inviting someone. I picked up the phone.

"How would you like to go skating tonight?"

"Go where?" asked the voice on the other end of the phone.

"Roller-skating," I said.

I went on to give the details.

"I want to know if you want to go skating with me," I repeated.

"Well, I think I might just do that," answered the voice. My mother's voice.

I can't think of anyone who loved roller-skating as a youngster more than my mother. She has talked about her skating experiences for as long as I can remember. My mother started skating when she was a young girl and in her teenage years spent five or six nights a week at the rink. But as she married and soon had four children to raise, she didn't have much time for her favorite hobby.

It had been a long time since Mama had skated, but I couldn't think of anyone in the world who would enjoy a night at the skating rink more than my mother.

She started out cautiously. She is, after all, old enough to be my mother. Mamaws have a hard time playing ball with grandsons with broken arms. She definitely didn't want to take any chances.

Before long, she had an audience.

"Why, Shirley Tobin, you're skating!" exclaimed one of the young mothers. She even called her mother-in-law to "come see!" But Mama wasn't just skating. She was gliding.

I tried to imitate my mother. I skated behind her and watched as she effortlessly sailed around the rink. As I mimicked her movements, I finally called out, "Mama, how do you do that?"

"Left, right, left, right," she said as her voice faded in the roar of the laughter and music.

But we both knew that it was much more than left, right. She had learned to skate as a child. She had been taught and encouraged, and when the time came for her to skate again after so many years, it was still in her. Her ability to skate had never left. And when she needed it, it all came back to her.

That's not the only thing my mother learned as a child. She is kind and compassionate. She is strong and unselfish. And she is faithful in her prayers and diligent in her study of God's Word.

Why? Because she was taught those things. She can still quote Bible verses that she learned as a girl. "Study to shew thyself approved unto God, a workman that needeth not to be ashamed, rightly dividing the word of truth" (2 Timothy 2:15, KJV).

It makes me think about what we are instilling in our children. When faced with peer pressure, will our boys remember the verses that their daddy has quoted over and over?

> Blessed is the man who does not walk in the counsel of
> the wicked or stand in the way of sinners or sit in the
> seat of mockers. For his delight is in the law of the Lord,
> and on His law he meditates day and night. Psalm 1:1–2

The Bible says, "Train up a child in the way he should go: and when he is old he will not depart from it" (Proverbs 22:6, KJV). Like my mother, each one of us is a reflection of the training we have received. People may look at our outsides, but they see our hearts. Don't be too busy. Train your children today.

Love keeps no record of wrongs

"Happy Anniversary!" called my husband.

This is January, I thought. *We were married in June*. But it didn't take me long to realize what he was talking about.

"Happy Anniversary to you too," I replied. "But you've got the wrong day. It's tomorrow."

Reaching for his calendar, he said, "Oh, I must have looked at the calendar wrong."

We acknowledge this anniversary every year. We don't make a big deal out of it, but this year we did figure out that it was the twenty-fifth anniversary of our first date, the day when two lives began the journey toward one, even though we weren't aware of it at the time.

I am thankful for the love that we share. But as with

most married couples, we don't have as much time for each other as we need. Responsibilities often pull us in different directions. Sometimes we take our frustrations out on each other. Sometimes we take each other for granted.

Relationships take work, whether it is a marriage, a parent/child relationship, or a friendship. And sometimes life episodes get in the way.

We were in a little shop on our honeymoon in Williamsburg, Virginia, when I saw two glass figurines, a boy and a girl, leaning toward each other with their hands behind their backs, lips puckered. With her blonde hair and his brown hair, they were us. They would make a wonderful sentimental souvenir of our honeymoon. I wanted them.

Unfortunately, my husband didn't.

"Aren't they cute?" I asked. "They look just like us."

"Let's go," he answered. "You don't need them."

Obviously, he had missed the point.

"I know I don't *need* them. I *want* them," I explained. "It's something we can keep forever, always reminding us of this special time. Look, $1.40 for both of them."

He finally gave in. Money wasted in his mind. Precious memories in mine.

Fast forward twenty years. As I opened the gift he gave me on our anniversary that year, I cried. The gift was Precious Moments figurines in wedding attire, the boy and girl pointing at their wedding rings, saying, "I still do."

"I realized how much you loved the figurines you bought on our honeymoon, and I've always felt a little guilty for giving you a hard time when you wanted to buy them," he confessed.

Unfortunately, I had a confession of my own. For twenty years, it is true, I had loved them. And I loved him. But sometimes he made me angry. Sometimes he didn't do things my way. So on those days, I use those figurines to pout. He had never noticed even though they were sitting on our dresser in our bedroom. Some days I turned her back to him. Sometimes I moved her away from him. Some days I hid her.

So I told him. He was shocked. But he began to watch the figurines. Life flowed smoothly for a while, and the little boy and girl stayed puckered, lips to lips. Until...

Well, it was football. A little boy whining as his daddy dragged him out the door and the mama feeling sorry for the little fellow. As soon as they walked out the door, I stomped up those steps, straight to our bedroom. I whirled that little girl figure across the dresser, turning her back to him, and moving her as far away from him as I could get her. I knew he would notice this time. *There*, I thought, *take that!*

But I couldn't leave them that way. They were lips to lips again before he came home, not only because I knew he would notice, but because "love is patient, love is kind. It is not rude, it is not self-seeking, it is not easily angered, it keeps no record of wrongs" (1 Corinthians 13:1–5).

So I choose to keep my little figurines face to face and puckered up these days. Oh, I still pout. But when God ordained and blessed our marriage, we promised to love and honor one another in good times and in bad times. And you know what? We still do.

Reviving our spiritual health

I was on my way home from a reading conference when my cell phone rang.

"Mom, could you stop by the grocery store?" asked my fifteen-year-old son.

"Sure," I answered. "What do you need?"

"Well, I need some buttermilk," he replied, "and could you get me some of that stuff in a can?"

I thought for a moment.

"Oh, do you mean Crisco?"

"Yeah, that's it. The flour is already in the bowl. I'm making biscuits."

I could get used to this. I remember how much I enjoyed the days when my oldest son had taken the Foods and

Nutrition course at school. He had made some delicious pizza. Now his brother was taking the same course and was anxious to try out some of the recipes that his teacher had given him.

The biscuits that he made for us that night were tender and fluffy. In fact, they were much better than the biscuits I make.

"Mom," he explained, "nutrition is a science. Because there is less protein in this brand of flour, there is less gluten. That's what holds the dough together. Since there is less gluten, biscuits are less likely to be tough. You work your biscuits too much, Mom. Don't handle them so much and they'll be softer."

I was impressed, not only with his biscuits, but with what he was learning about nutrition.

"Mom," he said one night as I put the supper on the table, "broccoli is good. But it really would have been better for us if you had left off the cheese."

As he opened the refrigerator later that evening, I saw him comparing the labels on two cartons of yogurt. He turned to me and asked, "Why would anyone eat this kind of yogurt when they could eat that kind and have much less fat and sugar?"

My boys have made some definite changes in their eating habits since they have taken the Foods and Nutrition course at school. They eat less fried foods. They watch their carbohydrate intake and eat lots of tuna for protein. They read labels and compare the vitamins and nutrients in their favorite foods. Not only do they watch what they eat, but they maintain physical health by participating in sports and weight training. We can see the results.

They are careful to keep their hands washed and their cooking surfaces clean. They have started checking out the sanitation grade in local restaurants because they know how important cleanliness is to health. They read books and magazines on health and nutrition.

My boys aren't the only ones who are working hard to make their physical bodies the best they can be. The local gyms are full of people with the same thing in mind. They spend hundreds of dollars on the right food and the right exercise equipment. They spend countless hours in the pursuit of the perfect physique. But is that enough?

Evidently not, because inside those nearly perfect bodies are some broken hearts. Inside those perfect bodies are some crushed spirits. Some of the same people that spend countless hours in the gym can't spare a couple hours on Sunday to nourish their spiritual selves. People who wouldn't dream of eating off a dirty plate think nothing of seeing a movie, watching a television show, or listening to music that dirties their minds and their souls.

Most of the schools are doing a good job of teaching our children about nutrition and physical health. We are challenged daily by advertisements and commercials to get healthy. But what about our spiritual health? What about the spiritual health of our children?

Maybe it's time we take some advice from King Solomon. "Eat honey my son, for it is good; honey from the comb is sweet to your taste. Know also that wisdom is sweet to the soul; if you find it, there is a future hope for you" (Proverbs 24:14).

Yes, physical health is a wonderful thing, but spiritual health is everything.

Finding the perfect peace

"Thank you for letting me come over, Aunt Donna." My nephew had come to spend the night with our boys. "I love to come to your house. It's so peaceful."

Peaceful? My idea of peaceful was a mountain cabin with rocking chairs on the front porch and a babbling brook flowing nearby. But our house?

There is never a quiet moment in our house. Every day is filled with boys who live here and boys who don't. Boys whose biological time clocks are not in sync with older people, like parents. Boys who can stay up all hours of the night. Boys who have loud music "systems," and boys who wrestle and play football in the house. Boys who eat all the time and leave crumbs everywhere.

As I thought back to the not-so-long-ago days when the boys were younger, I remembered precious times when three little boys were under foot. But peaceful? I haven't grown so old that my memory has faded that much.

I remember well the days when my husband had to use tweezers to pick popcorn kernels out of one boy's nose and green peas out of another's. I haven't forgotten the toilet paper trails that ran all over the house. We still have pictures of boys who were so caked with mud that we can't tell who is who.

I realize that as parents get older, they do tend to have "selective" memory. And I look forward to the day when I can remember only the good times. But right now I'm still refereeing fights and digging smelly socks out from under beds.

Not exactly a peaceful picture. And yet it was only a few weeks after my nephew had visited that a friend of my oldest son came over.

"You know, I think I'll just stay here," he said. "It's so peaceful."

I couldn't believe it. There was that word again.

I decided to grab this boy and question him.

"What do you mean, peaceful?"

He wasn't much help.

"Well, you know, just peaceful," he said.

I stood for a moment and looked around. I had a hard time finding anything in our house that wasn't glued, stapled, or taped back together. Yes, it wasn't hard to see that we had done a heap of living in this home.

I remembered the times that we had tried to have a few peaceful family minutes. Even our family devotional time is chaotic at times. When the boys were small, we were usually trying to hold at least one boy down while we read the Bible. And as they grew older, "Sit down and shut up, we're going to read the Bible," didn't exactly match our original intentions for family quiet time.

So what is it? What is this peace that the boys feel when they are in our home? It's definitely not an outside peace. Anyone who cares to listen in on our family will have an awfully hard time hearing the babbling brook when we're all talking at one time. But the peace is there. And after I thought awhile, it didn't take me long to figure it out.

Isaiah 26:3 (KJV) says, "Thou wilt keep him in perfect peace, whose mind is stayed on thee: because he trusteth in thee." No, it's not an outside peace. It's an inside peace. A peace between a Christian husband and wife that surpasses that of any other human relationship. A peace between parents and children who love and respect each other, pray for each other, and support each other. A peace between brothers who squabble on the outside but share an unbreakable bond of love. A peace that is not of this world, one that only God can give.

Just now, in fact, the boys come in to tell me that they are hungry again. So before the chaos sets in, I'll whisper a prayer for your family and mine, that, once again, the peace of God that surpasses all understanding will fill our hearts and minds today and every day.

Dealing with life's kinks

"What else can I do to help you?" asked my mother. Daddy was at a college football game, and Mama and I had spent a couple of hours shopping.

I really wanted to enjoy this time with my mother, but all I could think about were the mounds of dirty clothes that I had waiting at home. My husband was mowing the yard, and with one boy at the library and the other two at an amusement park, I knew that all the dirty piles would be waiting on me when I walked in the door.

"Your daddy won't be home until late tonight," Mama said, "so why don't I just go home with you and help you catch up on your work?"

I took my mother up on her offer. Between the fifth and

sixth loads of clothes, she had swept out the garage, emptied the trash, and dusted the den. She then asked, "What else?"

"Well, Mama, you could pair these socks." Somehow, that's one job that never gets done at our house. Ask a boy to fold a load of clothes, and he is always left with a handful of socks that don't match. So after weeks of tossing the leftover socks in a laundry basket, we had managed to accumulate quite a pile. So for the next half-hour, Mama paired socks.

I never imagined that life would be this way. I like things in order. I like a place for everything and everything in its place. I like the smell of pine cleaner. But you'd never know it these days. It's a good day if the sink is not piled to the ceiling with dirty dishes.

This unorganized, chaotic part of my life is definitely not what I had planned. I had planned to always be in control. I had planned to keep the refrigerator cleaned out. But with a full-time job, my church work, a husband, and two boys playing football and one playing soccer in the same season, I'm dogpaddling like crazy, just trying to keep my head above the water.

So I make a to-do list. I write down everything that I need to accomplish. I know exactly, down to the minute, how I must spend my day. Then the phone rings. A friend drops by. A student needs a little extra time. I'm called to a meeting at church. A kink in my plans.

Sometimes I feel sorry for myself and think that no one understands. But many do. And Jesus understands. When I think of the tasks that He faced during his short time on this earth, I can imagine that he felt pressure and frustration, too.

After feeding five thousand and calming the sea and healing the sick, Mark 7:24 says that "Jesus left that place and went to the vicinity of Tyre. He entered a house and did not want anyone to know it: yet he could not keep his presence a secret." He was tired. He needed some peace and quiet, away from the throngs of people who needed Him. But then came the kink in his plans. It was a woman whose little daughter was possessed by an evil spirit. She needed his help.

So what did Jesus do? Did he look at his to-do list and say, "Oops, you're not on my list today"? Of course not. After talking with Jesus, "She went home and found her child lying on the bed and the demon gone" (Mark 7:30). It was a change of plans for Jesus, but a change of life for the mother and her daughter.

Could it be that God is calling us to be more flexible in our lives? Could it be that those aggravating interruptions in our plans are actually divine interruptions, life-changing interruptions?

I don't think I'm quite ready to throw away my plan book at school or my to-do list at home, but I am praying that God's plans will guide me every day. Who knows? That one little interruption to my perfect plans might just change a life forever. And it may just begin with mine.

When apathy becomes intolerable

The smell of fresh bread hung in the air as the little boy walked into his grandparents' house. His nose reminded him that it had been a long time since he had eaten. As he entered the kitchen, he noticed that his grandma and grandpa were just sitting down to supper. His mouth watered as he looked at the delicious meal that his grandmother had prepared.

"Hello, Bobby," greeted his grandma. "Do you want something to eat?"

"I don't care," said the boy.

"Well, if you don't care then I don't care either," answered his grandpa. As his grandparents ate their meal, the boy stood and watched. And when it came time for him to go home that night, he went home hungry.

My daddy has told that story for as long as I can remember. I think he still feels hunger pangs when he remembers that night so long ago.

"But why didn't your grandmother insist that you have something to eat?" I've asked my dad. "They must have known that you were hungry." Maybe I didn't understand at first because we live in such a different time. When I was growing up, my parents insisted that we ask politely if we wanted something to eat or drink at our grandparents' house. We have also told our boys to "ask" before they go rummaging through their grandparents' cabinets and refrigerators.

But my dad was taught that it was impolite to ask for anything. He should wait until it was offered to him. And in this case, they did offer. But by "not caring," he did without.

That one missed meal made an impression on my dad that has lasted him a lifetime. And it is also a lesson that he has taught his own children as well. Daddy could accept our shortcomings, our mistakes, even our failures if we tried, but he could not, would not, tolerate our apathy.

And it's so subtle. How many good reputations have been ruined by careless attitudes? My son and I were discussing one of his classes at school the other day.

"You have less than two weeks to prepare for the end-of-course exam," I was saying. I went on to give him suggestions for studying and preparing for the test.

"Mom, you're talking about this like fighting fire, and all I'm doing is counting the days, trying to slide by."

"That's okay," I replied. "I thought you wanted to drive a

car some day. But I guess it's all right if we let your learner's permit to drive slide by."

I hope he gets the message loud and clear.

It's a message we've been trying to teach our children their whole lives. If you care about the little things, if you do the little things right, then the big things have a way of working themselves out. But if you don't care, you're digging yourself a hole that you can't pull yourself out of. Like the little girl who held up her hand to her mom's face and said, "Talk to the hand 'cause the ears don't hear." In other words, who cares?

The church of Laodecia had a similar attitude. In Revelation, John writes letters from the Lord to seven churches of believers in Asia Minor living at the end of the first century. Laodecia was the church that he referred to as being "lukewarm": "I know your works, that you are neither cold nor hot. I could wish you were cold or hot. So then, because you are lukewarm, and neither cold nor hot, I will vomit you out of my mouth" (Revelation 3:15–16).

I guess that's why I feel queasy every time I see a shirt with the word "whatever" across the front. It expresses an attitude that has crept into our schools, our churches, our world. It's an attitude that makes us straddle the fence. It makes us stand for nothing and fall for anything.

Sometimes I wonder just how much we are missing out on because we just don't care. A belly full of warm food? I have a feeling that it's more. Much more.

Christianity requires active searching

"Mom, could you come and help me?" My youngest son was standing in front of the pantry cabinet in the kitchen with the doors wide open. "I'm looking for chicken noodle soup," he said. "Why don't we ever have chicken noodle soup?"

It was a moment of dé já vu for me. I had been here before, seen this very scene—a boy standing in front of a cabinet with his hands on his hips, saying, "Mom, where did you put the soup?"

I walked over to the cabinet. It took me about two seconds to move a can of tomato soup over and reach behind it to pick up the chicken noodle soup.

"Your soup," I said, handing him the can. "Now why can't you do that?"

Without a moment's hesitation, he answered, "I don't look with my hands, Mom. I look with my eyes."

For the next few minutes I was silent, trying to process the volume of information in those few spoken words.

"I don't look with my hands," I repeated under my breath. That's it! That explained why I had spent the last twenty years of my life just looking for things, especially when the males in our family outnumber me four to one. It is obvious that it has been my job to be the finder of every lost item, the mover of anything that obscures from view the item of choice.

For all these years, I had wondered to myself, *Why is it that he can't move the bottle of vitamins and pick up the bottle of aspirin right behind it? What could possibly be so hard about moving the jar of mayonnaise in the refrigerator to see if the bottle of ketchup is behind it?* I could hear my mother's voice as she chided my brothers, "Why, if it had been a snake, it would have bitten you!"

Evidently, it takes my magic hand to find things in our house. If you ask the boys, I usually hide their things anyway. Why, just this week, I've lost tickets to a church supper (tickets that I don't remember seeing), a lead pencil, and a calculator, just to mention a few. I did admit to seeing the lead pencil and the calculator. My middle son was not happy when he had to go to calculus class without them.

"Mom, I left them right here in the kitchen," he said in an accusing tone when he came in from class that afternoon. That's right. He left them in my kitchen, so I must have been guilty.

"Let's see," I said. "Yes, I did see your things. That's right, your big brother was helping your little brother study for a math test last night, right here in the kitchen."

He was still blaming me until I made the little brother check his book bag, where he found two calculators and an extra lead pencil.

"I don't look with my hands, Mom. I look with my eyes." In other words, I don't do anything; I just stand there and expect it to just jump into my hands. I want something to happen. I want to eat chicken noodle soup, but not if I have to put too much effort into it. I'd rather have someone else do it for me.

Sound familiar? As Christians we want good things for ourselves and for others. But the Bible says,

> What good is it, my brothers, if a man claims to have faith but has no deeds? Can such faith save him? Suppose a brother or sister is without clothes and daily food. If one of you says to him, "Go, I wish you well; keep warm and well fed," but does nothing about his physical needs, what good is it? James 2:14–16

The Lord calls us to seek out the lost. Seeking calls for action. Just standing by with our hands on our hips, shaking our sympathetic heads will never bring anyone to the Lord. Maybe it's not as simple as lending a hand to find a can of soup. But then, maybe that is a step in the right direction.

Aging matters less if you have faith

"Well, how did you two manage to get a day together without the children?" The nice salesman smiled at my husband and me as we entered the furniture store that Saturday morning.

"Fact is," my husband answered, "our boys are almost grown. They're sixteen, eighteen, and twenty."

I smiled as the salesman's jaw dropped. I'd like to think that we really did look like the young couple that he hinted we were. But he was probably just a good actor wanting to sell some furniture that day. At least, that's what the boys said when we told them what the furniture man had said to us.

"Come on, guys," I said. "The man said that when he saw us come through the door, at first he thought that we were probably newlyweds."

"Oh, Mom, please," they groaned. "You can't be that gullible."

I guess not. The truth is, I know exactly how old I am. Oh, I keep my treadmill hot. I've even started lifting a few weights and shed a few pounds. I have my own stash of anti-wrinkle creams, and I use them faithfully every day. But time has a way of moving on. And boys have a way of bringing mothers back to reality.

I remember as a teenager riding to the grocery store with a neighbor who had just had a baby. The lady already had a grown son and was in her early forties at the time. When we got to the store, a lady walked up to her and admired her newborn.

"Are you the baby's grandma?" the lady asked.

I don't remember her exact reply, but I do remember the look she gave that woman. When we got in the car, she was still fuming.

"Well, I knew I wasn't a spring chicken, but I didn't know that I was an old hen!" she said loudly.

Now it's me who's no longer the spring chicken. As seasons go, I guess I'd have to say that my husband and I are in the fall of our lives. We're not newlyweds, not even close. In June, we'll celebrate twenty-five years of marriage, or a quarter of a century, the boys like to say. We're talking more about retirement. We're watching our sons grow and go away. Our last visit from our oldest son was less than twenty-four hours long, even though it had been more than a month since we had seen him. The middle one is making plans to go off to college soon, and the youngest one just got his driver's license and plans to drive off into the sunset as soon as we'll let him. At least for the next six months he'll have a nine o'clock curfew.

Solomon, the writer of Ecclesiastes, shares his thoughts on the matter of time in the third chapter of that book in the Bible.

> There is a time for everything and a season for every activity under heaven: a time to be born and a time to die, a time to plant and a time to uproot ... He has made everything beautiful in its time. Ecclesiastes 3:1–2, 11

I always thought that my grandmother was a beautiful lady, but I'll never forget the day that eighty-year-old lady looked in the mirror and said, "Who is that old woman? I don't even know her." Then she held up a picture of the young lady she once was and said, "This is me."

When I look in the mirror, I still see me. But I know if the good Lord lets me live to be my grandmother's age, one day there will be a different me in the mirror. This old body will age and wrinkle, slow down, and eventually quit.

But oh, that my soul will keep on singing. Even through the cold, dark days of winter, my love for my Savior will sustain me. The promise of a new body and life eternal will be my greatest hope.

In the end, that's all that matters anyway. So, boys, you're right. Not even your mama can stay young forever. But that's okay, because, boys, it is well with my soul.

Please bring them home safely

Ah, they're back. I could hear the muffled voices and the familiar thump of the basketball on the concrete. I had been watching for them, and, sure enough, they were right on time.

They had started out almost two hours before on their adventure. "They" were my youngest son and two of his cousins. My son had taken a long walk with his dad in the woods the day before and couldn't wait to show his cousins what he had seen.

"It is so cool," he had told me. "It reminds me of another world, a place from long ago." So when I heard the boys bound down the stairs that Sunday afternoon, I knew what they were up to.

"Where are you boys going?" I asked.

"We're going to that dam, Mom," my son replied.

Immediately, my mind's eye conjured up the image that he had described the day before.

"It's huge, Mom, big giant rocks stacked one on top of the other, maybe twenty feet high and a creek that looks more like a little river," he had said.

Yes, I know they're teenagers, but still, I was concerned. I began to fire questions.

"How long will you be gone? Which way do you plan to go? Did you get the two-way radios? You're not going in your church clothes, are you? I hope you know that you're not taking that thing in your hand."

My son began to answer my list of questions.

"Well, maybe I will change my clothes. We could take your cell phone, Mom. This old thing? It's just a machete. I took it with me yesterday."

I was just getting ready to retaliate when I heard a quiet comment from behind me, out of earshot of the boys.

"Just let them be boys," the voice said. My husband's voice. I took a deep breath. Good grief, it was a romp in the woods.

"How long will you be gone?" I asked.

"I have a watch," my nephew said. "Will four fifteen be okay?"

"Four fifteen will be just fine," I replied.

And four fifteen it was. I met them at the door with cold drinks and listened as they told me about their adventure.

"We would have stayed longer, but we told you that we'd be back," they said. "And we always do what we say, well, mostly."

And mostly, they do. So why is it so hard for me to let them go? For one thing, I've never been a boy. I never played cowboys and Indians. I never had a desire to hunt or fish or even get dirty. I never played army with plastic guns.

Maybe that's another reason. For almost four months, I have been e-mailing my husband's cousin in Bagram, Afghanistan. He is an Apache helicopter pilot, and during this time he has shared with me his own stories of war. With his words, he has taken me to the caves of Kandahar as he searches for members of Al Qaida. He has shared his fears and frustrations and his love for a little daughter back home. And every single time I talk to him, my heart aches for his mother. It wasn't so long ago that he was her little boy, romping through the woods, doing all the things that boys do. But it's late now, and she has no idea when he will come home.

The Bible talks of wars and rumors of war. We pray for peace, and yet we know that turmoil is inevitable in a sinful world. There is one promise that we claim, however, whether the doubt and fear is in our hearts or if we are standing in the midst of it.

In Hebrews, God says, "Never will I leave you; never will I forsake you." So we say with confidence, "The Lord is my helper; I will not be afraid. What can man do to me?" (Hebrews 13:5–6) "Therefore, put on the full armour of God, so that when the day of evil comes, you may be able to stand your ground, and after you have done everything, to stand" (Ephesians 6:13).

Today, I claim God's promise of protection for my children and yours, whether he's off to kindergarten for the first time or she's off to college or they're off to war. May the loving God of peace wrap His arms around you and hold your precious children in the palm of His hand. And bring them home, Lord. Please, bring them safely home.

God is watching,
even when big brothers aren't

It was broad daylight. My youngest son and I were running errands, trying to get him ready for a youth retreat at the beach. We had picked up snacks and were on our way home when I remembered something.

"You're supposed to take a flashlight," I said.

"I don't have one," he answered. "We need to stop and get one."

"I'll just run in the dollar store. Hey, look, there's your brother's car," I remarked offhandedly. "He must be working out at the gym. Are you coming in with me?"

"Nah," he answered. "I'll wait out here."

I had been in the store less than five minutes when he charged in. He was red-faced and sweaty.

"Hurry, Mom. You won't believe what I did!"

I hurriedly paid for the flashlight and walked out with him.

"What in the world?" I began. He was so proud, the youngest of three boys, always ready to stand his ground, ready to pounce like a tiger if need be. There is never a dull moment with this boy, and he likes it that way.

I looked over at his oldest brother's car. The front windshield was covered with all kinds of papers. Held securely by the windshield wipers were flyers from events long gone and free "take one" newspapers. There were wrappers and advertisements and receipts, even an empty French fry box. The boy had trashed his big brother's car in the parking lot of the gym where his brother was working out.

"Why?" I asked.

He was almost too excited to answer. "Oh, I wish I could hide and be here when he comes out! This is so cool. He's going to think it was one of his buddies or maybe even a girl. I can just see his face now."

All the way home, he talked about his prank. He kept speculating on who his brother would suspect.

"Did it occur to you that he could have looked out of the window and seen you?" I asked.

"No way," he answered.

"How about witnesses? Don't you think that someone saw you make that mess?"

"Lots of guys with bulging muscles went by, but they didn't care," he replied.

"Did you ever think that the bright blue Superman shirt that you're wearing might be a dead giveaway?" He wasn't buying any of this. He was still convinced he had pulled off the prank of the century. He was waiting in the kitchen when his brother walked in from the gym. Without a second's hesitation, the big brother walked straight to the little brother, laughed, and smeared his sweaty T-shirt into his brother's face.

"How did you know?" asked the prankster. "Did you see me?"

"Well, actually," he replied, "it was the receipt for the movies we rented last night with Mom's name on it. I knew Mom wouldn't trash my car. So it had to be you."

Rats. Outsmarted again. And he never saw it coming.

But the part that still surprises me is that he did it in broad daylight and never expected to be caught. Of course, it was just an innocent prank and no harm was done. But what about the pranks that aren't so innocent? What about our actions that are in direct disobedience to the Word of God?

The second chapter of Exodus tells such a story. In broad daylight, an angry Moses, after glancing around and seeing no one, killed an Egyptian and hid him in the sand. When questioned about the killing, the Bible says that Moses "was afraid and thought, 'What I did must have become known'" (Exodus 2:14). Then Moses ran for his life.

People used to hide. They used to be sneaky. But it seems these days that more people do their sinning in broad daylight, leaving careless clues. And most of them never give a thought to being caught.

Proverbs 15:3 says, "The eyes of the Lord are everywhere, keeping watch on the wicked and the good."

So remember, little brother, you can run, but you can't hide. Even if big brother isn't watching, you can be sure that God is.

God makes a way
for mothers of the world

"Aunt Donna," my nephew said as I answered the phone. He was sweet-talking me, and I knew it. "Would it be all right if I spend the night at your house this weekend?"

"Of course you can," I assured him. "You can come over any time you want. We love to have you here."

I was telling the truth. Since my oldest son has been away at college, I find myself opening my arms a little wider to my younger sons' friends and my teenage nephews. With my middle son making plans to leave home next year too, I am reminded that my time to mother a house full of boys will not last forever. In fact, the light at the end of the tunnel that I had looked forward to as an exhausted young mother is looking more like the glare of a locomotive ready to crash into me at any moment. And I don't like it.

So I hang on to the boys with all my might. All the boys. When they want to spend the night at our house, I change the sheets and fluff the pillows. When they want food, I order pizza, serve them walnut chocolate chip cookies straight from the oven, and bake cream cheese pound cakes. I make pancakes and omelets, or "Momlets," as they like to call them, for breakfast. My husband and I make special trips to Krispy Kreme to buy chocolate cream-filled doughnuts for one of our nephews because we know they're his favorite.

I find old toothbrushes to scrub wax out of crevices when they wash their cars at our house. I scour the mud glops off the floor when they track it in from their treks in the woods. I wash other boys' clothes and hold my tongue when they occasionally leave a half-full drink can on the nightstand in a bedroom.

I smile and welcome them when they want to have band practice at our house on Saturday afternoons.

"No, it's not too loud," I say to the boy who has just spent the last half hour lugging his drum set up the stairs to a room directly over my kitchen, praying that the ceiling fan won't crash on the table.

Yes, I love them all, my sons and other mothers' sons. I have always prayed that God would put someone in the lives of my sons when they couldn't or wouldn't hear my counsel. I would like to think that God would use me in the life of even one of the boys who spends so much time in our home.

I was running an errand for one of my boys recently when an older gentleman began to talk to me. I was at a flea market on a beautiful Saturday morning. I was in a hurry and on a mission, looking for bargain-priced cartridges for my son's razor. The gentleman was on a mission too, he told me, looking for a bargain just as I was.

"I'm here to buy flowers for my son's grave," he said. "They have beautiful flowers at a good price."

I was so shocked at his words that I didn't know what to say. "But you're not supposed to have to bury your son," I think I mumbled.

I was reminded of another mother and another son. I can imagine that Mary, the mother of Jesus, would understand my mother's heart as I desperately cling to each son. I imagine that Mary baked her boy's favorite foods and welcomed his friends into her home. She probably washed her share of dirty, dusty clothes and endured the loud, good-natured horseplay of teenage boys. I'm sure that her home was a safe place, a haven from the storms of the world to many boys in her day.

But in the midst of her happy home, there was heartache, which eventually led to a mother's heart broken at the foot of a cruel cross.

Yet even then, God made a way for Mary. As He was dying, Jesus made sure that His mother would be cared for. One of her son's friends, a young man she no doubt had loved and welcomed into her home, would now welcome her into his home and his heart. He would love her as his own mother (John 19:26–27).

I know that God will make a way for me too. Even when the boys are grown and gone, I have a feeling I'll still be doing my share of mothering. For as long as there are lost boys and girls in this world, there will be other mothers praying for someone to come along when their own sons and daughters don't or won't hear their counsel. And who knows? Maybe God will let that *someone* be me.

The many blessings
of a love that's unimaginable

It was noon when I put the plate of pancakes in front of my middle son. We were out of school that day, and he had slept late. As he plopped down at the table, he looked at me and grinned.

"She says I'm spoiled," he said. He had just talked to his girlfriend, mentioning the fact that his mom was making him pancakes for lunch since he slept through breakfast.

"She's right," I said. "You are. I bet you can't even count all your blessings. All of us need a reminder once in a while."

My husband had just walked in from work and caught the end of the conversation.

"Go get that book," he said to me. Turning to our nineteen-year-old son, he continued, "Mama's going to read you a book while you eat your pancakes."

Our son looked at his dad like he had finally gone off the deep end. "What is he talking about?" he asked me as he surveyed his dad with suspicious eyes.

"Just sit and listen," his dad instructed.

I knew the book. In fact, I had just read it to my adult Sunday school class as part of the lesson a few weeks ago. Obviously, its powerful message had made just as much of an impact on my husband as it had me. As I left to get the book, I could still hear the banter from the kitchen. Our son was even more confused when I returned with a green picture book, a picture of an apple tree and a little boy on the front.

"Now, read it like you would in class," my husband told me. "Mama's going to hold it up so you can see the pictures," he said, looking over at our grown boy.

By this time, our son was too confused to ask any more questions. He just sat back and listened, waiting to see what would come next.

"'*The Giving Tree*,' by Shel Silverstein," I announced. "Once there was a tree … and she loved a little boy."

The story goes on to tell of a little boy who, every day, ate the tree's apples, swung from her branches, and slid down her trunk. The tree loved the little boy and was glad to give him anything she had to give to make him happy. She loved watching him grow and play. It was the boy's happiness that brought her joy.

But as the years passed, the boy spent less and less time with the tree. He began to search for his own way in the world, only calling on the old tree when he needed something. First he needed money, so the tree gave him her apples to sell to make money. Next, she gave him her branches so he could build a house. Finally, she gave him her trunk so that he could make a boat and sail away in search of happiness.

In the end, the boy is a tired old man. He returns to the tree, which has nothing left to give but an old stump for sitting and resting. The boy finally realizes that is exactly what he needs.

"And the tree was happy," I finished. "The end."

"That is the saddest first-grade story I've ever heard," my son said as I closed the book. Then, after a moment, "Mama, you're the tree, and I'm the boy," he groaned.

He's right about that. I've been that old tree, just giving and giving. I have especially felt like the tree in more recent years as my sons have grown. But I've been the boy too, taking. and taking some more, not realizing the magnitude of the gifts that I have received. Not thanking those who have been the "giving trees" in my life, those who gave for the pure joy of seeing me happy, who put my well-being above their own.

Every time I read that story it makes me think of another book that I've read. It reminds me of a gift greater than I could ever give, the greatest gift that I have ever received. John 3:16 begins like this, "For God so loved the world that He gave … "

As I looked at the boy eating his pancakes that day and thought about his brothers, I said the verse a little slower, drinking in the love that the Father has lavished on me. I can't imagine, no, I really can't imagine a love so great that I would give any one of my sons. And yet, God offered the gift of eternal life by giving His one and only son—for me, for you.

A stack of pancakes doesn't seem like much of a gift in comparison. Neither does a hug or a gentle pat on the back or a card or a phone call. But mixed with God's love, even the smallest gifts can be the greatest.

Our actions should reflect the Father

Ah, vacation.

For the first time, my extended family was taking a vacation together. There would be sixteen of us all together, including six teenage boys and a two-year-old. What could be more relaxing?

My parents camped while the rest of us rented our own family villas inside the campground. Each of us decided how we were going to spend the week. My sister could sun on the beach all day while I floated blissfully around the lazy river. Some played golf while others read books or rode bicycles.

We were all doing our own thing. Until Wednesday, that is. That's when the adults decided that "The Clampetts" should go to town. We planned to go to dinner together and to a show at the Alabama Theater.

Teenage boys don't have much in common with their parents, but for once, everyone was agreeable. Eating is always fine with them, and the show didn't seem so bad, until we told them we were going to wear the shirts.

That's right, the shirts. When we arrived at the camp-ground, my brother and his wife presented each family member with a light blue T-shirt with a pirate embroidered in the upper left corner with the words "The Bob Tobin 2002 Family Reunion." On the back was the word "PIRATELAND," with all our names listed underneath.

Before we left for town, we talked a camper into snapping pictures of us in our matching shirts. For most of us, it was a proud moment. It didn't matter that some of our shirts were a little big. Most of us weren't trying to make a fashion statement anyway. But some of us were. And believe me, the shirts were cramping their style.

Still, there wasn't a lot of traffic, just a few golf carts, with people smiling as we posed for the camera. Not so bad.

But then there was the restaurant. The teenagers who had been seeking attention from every girl on the beach were suddenly trying to crawl into the woodwork.

"Oh, do you work at Pirateland?" strangers asked, or, "A family reunion, how nice."

After dinner, we were on to the theater where the people were dressed to impress, especially the girls. My eighteen-year-old nephew commented that he had never seen so many good-looking girls congregated in one place at the beach and here he was, dressed liked his papaw's twin.

Of course, there is always an entertainer in the bunch. We have two. I just happen to be the sister of one and the mother of the other. After reminding my youngest son for the umpteenth time to behave, he had finally had enough.

"What's the big deal, Mom? Why does Papaw care so much how I act tonight?"

"Could it be this?" I asked, pointing to the words on his shirt. "That is Papaw's name. Tonight everything you do and say is a reflection of him."

It made me think of the other name that we, as Christians, carry around. Every day we are to be a reflection of God and His love. I'm afraid that some of us who carry the name of Jesus in our hearts are shaming Him with our actions. If we are to be the living, breathing image of Jesus Christ in this world today, then we need to start paying attention to what we say and do.

The Bible says: "Even a child is known by his actions, by whether his conduct is pure and right" (Proverbs 20:11). Whether I am honoring my earthly father or my Heavenly Father, my purpose is the same. I should reflect his love. I should make him proud to call me his child.

It will probably be a long time before we can talk six teenage boys into dressing like their parents again. But we will all carry our fathers' names every day. And maybe, just maybe, the matching blue shirts will be a reminder for us to honor them in everything we say and do.

His power is made perfect in weakness

"I can't believe I'm waiting in this line again," I moaned silently to myself.

The pharmacy line was long, and I could think of a hundred other things that I would rather be doing. But today I had no choice. I needed to pick up the medicine before the pharmacy closed, and at least a dozen other people obviously had the same idea. So I waited, lost in thoughts of prescription plans and deductibles when suddenly, I felt a tap on my shoulder.

"You can't be waiting on medicine for yourself," the lady in line behind me said. "You must be getting medicine for someone else. You look like the picture of health to me."

I don't know if I jumped because her words jolted me out of my thoughts or if I was surprised that she, a perfect stranger, told me precisely what she was thinking. I know people like her, people who never make you guess their opinion or wonder what they are thinking. They don't mince words. They don't hold back. They tell you exactly what is on their mind every time.

I shook the startled look off my face and smiled. "Well, you're right this time," I said. "I'm waiting to pick up my son's prescriptions today. But you'd be surprised how many times I stand in this line for myself."

I was flattered by the fact that she thought that I looked like the "picture of health." But what a person observes on the outside isn't always an indication of what is going on inside. Believe me, there have been times in the past when I wouldn't have wanted to be anywhere near this woman who spoke her mind so freely. But she was right in the fact that I have worked hard to transform my ever-aging body.

For the past two years, I have been much more careful about what I eat, concentrating on portion control and healthier choices. I exercise every day. I am more confident in my smaller-sized clothes, and I hope I can maintain my more physically fit body. But believe me, I am far from the picture of perfect health that the woman saw that day when she looked at me.

Without going into the details of my medical history, suffice it to say that syringes and finger-pricking and pill-taking are part of my life every day. I, like the Apostle Paul, also have a thorn in the flesh. I, like Paul, have pleaded with the Lord to take it away from me. But as the Lord replied to

Paul, he has also said to me, "My grace is sufficient for you, for my power is made perfect in weakness" (2 Corinthians 12:9a). Therefore, like Paul, I "will boast all the more gladly about my weaknesses, so that Christ's power may rest on me. That is why, for Christ's sake, I delight in weaknesses, in insults, in hardships, in persecutions, in difficulties. For when I am weak, I am strong" (2 Corinthians 12:9b-10).

I can't help but think of a man I met recently. He was not the picture of perfect health. In fact, I have seen few so obviously diseased on the outside. There was not a square inch of his exposed skin that was smooth. His body was ravaged with tumors, covering his face, neck, and arms. As we talked, he explained the terrible disease that had afflicted him for years. He told of his love for children and their innocent questions and how he tried to explain this hideous disease to them. But he also spoke of the cruel comments that adults made and their insensitivity to his condition.

It made me thankful that my disease doesn't show. I hide it well. If I didn't tell you, you might never guess. But it is there, nonetheless. It afflicts me every second of every day. Some days, it determines where I can go and what I can do. It is an inconvenience every day and, on the worst days, it is a black cloud hanging over my future.

But that is only on the worst days. It is also an exercise in endurance. It is a test of strength and a lesson in discipline. Yes, it is a thorn in my flesh, but I will not question God's will and authority in my life.

I know that God could take my disease away if He chose to. I believe, like the lepers of old, God could give the tumored man a perfect complexion. But until that day,

I will not ask, "Why me, Lord?" Instead, I will ask, "Why not me?" And I pray that God will use even my afflictions for His glory so I can be the picture of health where it really matters ... way down deep in my soul.

To be good at the game, you must play by the rules

"We're bored, Aunt Donna," announced my nephew as the trio streaked through our front door.

It was Saturday afternoon, and my youngest son and two of his cousins had been to the pool. The sky was overcast, but the pool was crowded anyway, they said, too crowded to swim.

"So we played Ping-Pong," they explained, "and then we remembered that you had a Ping-Pong table in the basement, so we decided to come here."

They were right. We did have a Ping-Pong table in the basement... in a box. That Ping-Pong table had been a gift to our family many, many years ago from my parents. We had hinted about how much we would like to have a table some day. They had taken the hint. But somehow, the table had managed to find its way into a corner of our basement, and the box had never been opened. We had originally planned to clear out the perfect place for the table and set it up. But the boys became interested in other things like football, Scouts, and skateboarding. So we never did.

Looking back, I guess I was the one who had wanted it the most anyway.

Coming from a family of athletes, I was the only one who didn't have an athletic bone in my body. Oh, I was a cheerleader in the days when all you had to do was yell loud and jump around. And, of course, there was the time I won second place in a big splash contest at a swim meet. I don't even like to remember that one.

But Ping-Pong. Now that was a sport that even I could play. I remember playing for hours at my aunt's house as a teenager. My cousins and I played a game called "Round Table," and I was really pretty good at it. A dozen or so of us would gather around the table and wait our turn to hit the ball while racing around the table. If you missed, you were eliminated. I usually managed to stay in the game longer than most of the others. Or at least I like to remember it that way.

So the bored boys went to work. Before long, they had assembled the table, cleared a spot, and were playing my favorite game.

Later that evening after all the boys had left, I decided to challenge my husband to a game of Ping-Pong. I knew I might be a little rusty, but I didn't have any doubt that after a few volleys, I'd soon be as competitive as ever. I was right. *It's like riding a bicycle,* I thought to myself as I returned my husband's serve. *I'm good at this game.* My smile covered my whole face.

"I'm ready," I soon told him.

"Ready?" he asked.

"Yes," I explained, "ready for a real game, ready to keep score."

"Are you sure?" he asked.

"I'm sure," I answered. "I'll serve."

It was really fun ... at first. But it didn't take me long to figure out that playing for fun, just hitting the ball back and forth, was a whole lot different than playing by the rules.

"I don't want to sound like a crybaby or anything, but could we switch sides?" I asked my husband after losing the first several games. Soon I suggested that it might be time to trade paddles.

"Maybe I'm just too short," I finally decided after another loss.

"Short?" my husband asked.

"Yeah, you know, I need a longer arm span."

He groaned.

I couldn't believe it. I had really convinced myself that I was a good Ping-Pong player. And I was, as long as I was living up to my own standards of what "good" was. But when we pulled out the rulebook ... well, let's just say I have a long way to go to be as good as I thought I was.

Sound familiar? How many church members are making their own rules? Let's see, I gave more money than he did, went to church more times this month than she did, and even volunteered to help out with Vacation Bible School. That means I'm a pretty good Christian, right?

Maybe. But there's more to it than that. It depends on who is Lord of your life and whose standards you're trying to live up to. Lots of people like to call themselves Christians. They even play a pretty good game of saying the right things and doing good deeds. But how many of us are really playing by the real rules? God's rules, that is.

As for Ping-Pong, I've lost every game so far. But that's okay. I keep playing by the rules, and the more I play, the better I play. Because whether it's a game of Ping-Pong or the game of life, I have decided to hold myself to the highest standard. That's the only way to victory.

It's time, and I'm not ready

I've heard it for years. Before you know it, they'll be gone. Enjoy every minute.

And I have. Not that every minute has been easy. I was a stay-at-home mother of three boys. There were days when my husband would come home from work to find me crying from exhaustion.

Some days the boys took mud baths. Other days they stuck green peas up their noses. There was never a dull moment.

I am so blessed to have been able to stay at home with my boys. My heart is full of memories of that precious time. Somehow I wish we could have lingered together a little longer. But time has a way of moving on, as it should.

I know that my growing boys have many opportunities waiting just around the corner. And as it was when they were learning to take those first steps on their own, I know that it is time for this mother to let go once again. But instead of the baby steps that I am used to calling out for them to take in our old favorite game "Mother, May I?" someone else is doing the calling. And he's calling out giant steps.

Especially to my oldest son. In less than a month he will graduate from high school. His senior year has flown by in a blur of activity. He has worked hard and been successful. I peeped over his shoulder the other day to see the letter that he was writing to his classmates. As senior class president, I noticed that he stressed that graduation was not an end, but a beginning. Maybe he was writing that letter to his Mom too.

He took a giant step last week. He was invited to spend the night with a host in a dorm at a large university. The director of undergraduate admissions spoke to us when we arrived. Again and again he emphasized a liberal education.

"Employers want well-rounded employees," he said. "We encourage all groups to voice their opinions" (*Opinions that I have spent my life trying to shield from my sons,* I thought to myself).

Students were taken to special sessions while parents were given personal tours of the campus. As we toured, a young woman thrust a flyer out to my husband as he walked by, announcing a video series introducing The Supreme Master Somebody who would enlighten those who wanted to find out where they came from and to remember their mission on earth and to discover the secrets of the universe.

Then there was the message in the center of campus

from a fraternity that said, "I'd rather reign in *hell* than serve in *heaven*."

That's when I knew. My job as that boy's mother is far from over. I have spent nearly eighteen years protecting him. I held his hand when he tried to dart across the street. I read him Bible stories and taught him to pray. And if he decides to walk on that campus to live away from home for the first time, if my arms are no longer long enough to wrap around him, my prayers will still have a direct line to God the Father.

I will pray for him daily, and I will say to my son,

> Be strong in the Lord and in His mighty power.
> Therefore put on the full armor of God, so that when
> the day of evil comes, you may be able to stand your
> ground, and after you have done everything, to stand.
> Ephesians 5:10, 13

No, I'm not ready. I probably won't ever be. But I am thankful for the peace that passes all understanding, the peace that allows me to let go and let God work in the lives of my boys. And with God directing the steps, even when He calls out the giant steps, I can answer my son boldly, knowing that our heavenly Father holds him in His loving hands.

"Mother, may I?"

"Yes, you may."

Following in the footsteps of a beloved aunt

The Christmas Eve service had just ended. The people in the congregation were mingling and talking, wishing each other a Merry Christmas, when I felt the strong arms of my oldest son wrap around me. I was still at the piano where I had just finished playing "Silent Night." I had played that song hundreds of times, but this year the silence of this holy night brought on a flood of tears that I couldn't stop.

"It's so hard for me," I cried.

"I think it's hard for all of us, Mama," he said.

I had tried not to look up during the service. In our church, the organ and the piano face each other on either side of the choir loft. My beautiful white-haired aunt usually joined me as we played the songs together. I had learned through the years to keep my eyes on her almost as much as I kept them on my music, because with a nod of her head, she directed me as I played. But this year, the organ was silent.

"Let me show you something," I told my son as I led him to the organ.

"Were those her shoes?" he asked.

"Yes," I replied. "I bet you didn't know that every Sunday for as long as I remember, she would slip off her Sunday shoes and put on these old shoes to play the pedals on the organ."

I found out later from my uncle that the shoes had indeed been there as long as I had thought. In fact, he told me that right after I was born, while he was in the military, someone had sent him a picture of my aunt's feet, just her feet, in a pointy-toed pair of shoes similar to those. I wondered if it could have been the same pair.

I couldn't get the shoes, or the lady who belonged to them, off my mind. I had been at the hospital the night before, along with many other family members. My aunt and uncle had never had children of their own, but they had parented so many nieces and nephews that any one of us could have been mistaken for a son or daughter. So we were all there when she had taken her last breath in the loving arms of her husband, my uncle.

Now we knew without a doubt that she was at last in the loving arms of her Heavenly Father.

After the funeral, I finally had a chance to speak to my uncle about the shoes.

"I was afraid someone would throw them away," he said, "so I went to get them this morning. Here, take them."

"I'll give them back," I promised.

So I took the shoes home and set them at the foot of my bed. For days, people had said, "Now it's up to you, Donna, to fill her shoes." She had told me at the end of the summer that she felt that the Lord had been grooming me for years to take over where she left off. And for months, her words had echoed in my head.

But how, Lord? She was so faithful, so loving and encouraging. I could never be even close to the spiritual, godly lady that she was.

"I'll prove it to you, Lord," I said through my tears. I was crying so hard that I could hardly see as I slipped my feet into her shoes. "They're too big! I told you, Lord, I can't fill her shoes." I sobbed. It was almost immediately that I felt my Heavenly Father's arms wrap tightly around me.

"I'm not asking you to," I heard Him say. "I'm asking you to follow in her footsteps, to walk with Me daily, as faithfully as she did."

I knew I could do that. She had taught me my whole life how beautiful it was to walk in the steps of the Savior. As a child, I had followed her about her chores at home and at church. She had prayed for me daily. To walk in her footsteps was the least I could do.

And so, until we meet again, my sweet Betty Jean, you play that celestial organ and lead that heavenly choir. In the meantime, I'll be following in your footsteps. I know you wouldn't have it any other way.

Relying on faith to weather crisis in our lives

"You need to eat," my husband nudged me gently. We had just left the hospital, and I still felt dull and dazed. I tried to think of the last time I had eaten, but I couldn't remember. Again, his gentle voice called me out of my deep thoughts as I tried to make sense of what he was saying.

"We can't let ourselves get weak physically," he said. "We can't take care of him if we don't take care of ourselves," he said as he turned into the parking lot of a restaurant.

I knew he was right. We were exhausted. What we had thought would be a relaxing vacation had turned into a desperate ride from a motel in Virginia to a hospital near home. Our youngest son was very sick, and we needed the medical care of doctors we could trust. After being treated in the hospital at home, he had been transferred to a larger hospital. We were assured by everyone we talked to that he was getting the best medical care possible. I knew that. But the child whom I had carried in the womb for nine months and in my heart for more than seventeen years was hurting. And I couldn't make the hurt go away.

So I sat, staring at the food in front of me, willing myself to eat. I repeated every Bible verse that I could think of that had brought me through times of trouble in the past.

"I can do all things through Christ which strengtheneth me" (Philippians 4:13, KJV).

"When I am afraid I will trust in you" (Psalm 56:3).

Once again, I claimed Jeremiah 29:11 for my son in the name of Jesus: "'For I know the plans I have for you,' declares the Lord, 'plans to prosper you and not to harm you, plans to give you a hope and a future.'" I called out to the Lord to protect him with the full armor of God so that he could stand his ground against the spiritual forces of evil in this world, that he would take up the shield of faith and the breastplate of righteousness. I claimed Psalm 91 and the promise that God has made to our family through his Word that He would send his angels concerning us and He will guard us and protect us, even in times of trouble. And I reminded myself that God will never, ever allow more burdens on us than we can bear.

Yet as I write these words, I feel the dark night of the soul deep within me. As my tears fall on the open Bible in my lap, I can only hang onto God and His promises. I have heard the kindness and concern in the nurses' voices as they keep me informed of my son's condition. I have prayed that in the times I am not allowed to be with him that God would not only send an army of angels to protect him, but one special angel to pat him on the head and to rub his back and to whisper words of comfort in his ear. I know that God has answered my prayer.

It is a hard journey. But I am reminded, as I have been in times of trouble and heartache with my boys, that I cannot possibly know what God might have to allow my sons to go through to get them to the place where He can use them. So as we face days of uncertainty, I know that God will carry my youngest son through these days, just as He is carrying me and the rest of our family in His loving arms of comfort and peace.

In the meantime, I am expected to go about everyday life. So for a few minutes today, I must think about the son who will celebrate his twenty-second birthday on a medical mission trip in Mexico next week. He had planned to go later, but circumstances have made it so that he must leave two weeks earlier than expected. Then I must think of the middle son. He is supposed to move into an apartment next week where he will be going to college. He needs a computer and a bed to sleep in. I will think about that tomorrow.

But today I will pray for complete healing. I will pray for protection. I will hang on to the words of encouragement from my family and friends. I will ask you to pray for my son and for our family. I believe that there is nothing on earth more powerful than the prayers of God's people. I will rest in the shadow of the Almighty and have faith that the Lord will work a mighty miracle in the life of our precious child. And yes, like Elijah, I will eat.

Grandma gave me many things, including a needed lesson

We had been taught that it was not polite to ask, but we knew we really didn't have to ask. Grandma had a way of knowing exactly what we wanted anyway.

One by one, whether we had been picking blackberries, sipping honeysuckles, or climbing the pink mimosa tree in her front yard, the grandchildren would make their way into her dark, damp old house. We were careful not to stretch our palms wide open as we passed our parents. That would be too obvious. But as we made our way inside, Grandma knew. While the adults visited in her sitting room, Grandma excused herself to her bedroom, where we followed, knowing we were only moments away from a special treat.

She kept her money wrapped in a handkerchief in a change purse that she tucked deep inside her big black purse. As she opened the wardrobe to pull out her purse, we could hardly wait. She counted out the money that we needed, and a little extra, of course, and sent us on our way.

We soon returned with big smiles and bright red tongues. The giant cherry slushy drinks from the store down the street were exactly what thirsty little grandchildren wanted after a long, hot afternoon of fun at Grandma's house.

My grandmother never had much money, and that weekly afternoon treat probably stretched her budget. She could have sent us to the kitchen for a drink of water after our romps outside. But Grandma was a giver. She set an example of "doing without" when it came to her family. She would rather give to us than to keep anything for herself.

As a child, I really didn't think much about it. Grandma gave, I took. But as I grew older, I began to see things in a more "adult" way. I began to think that Grandma was not very practical in her giving.

When I was in college, I began to take Grandma on her weekly trip to the grocery store. It didn't make sense when she tried to give me the carton of orange juice that she had just bought for herself.

"No, Grandma," I'd say. "You keep it for yourself. I don't need the juice." Besides that, I probably earned as much money at my part-time job as Grandma got in her Social Security check.

I began to feel guilty when she tried to give me gifts that other people had given her and aggravated when she tried to put "gas" money in my pocket as I was leaving.

So for a long time, I fussed when Grandma tried to give me things. I refused her gifts time and time again. Sometimes I hurried away from her house just so I didn't have to go through the ordeal of saying, "No, Grandma. I don't need it. I don't want it. You can't afford it. Keep it for yourself."

I kept that adult, "practical" attitude for years. Grandma had taught me the importance of giving with a cheerful heart, and I could do that with ease. But somehow, I neglected her other lesson. My practical, sensible self had missed the lesson on graciously, gratefully receiving.

Maybe that is because, compared to many others, my needs have been relatively few. My family has been comfortable and healthy. I have depended on my parents and then my husband in times when I have been unable to provide for myself. But in recent months, circumstances in my life and in the lives of those I love have made me weak and vulnerable and needy, calling out to Jesus with all my heart and soul.

That is when they came with gifts to our family. People sent meals and gift certificates. They prayed for us and mailed us cards and called to tell us that they were here for us anytime, day or night. Although there are still moments when I want to huddle in the darkness and cry, when I think of their gifts, I think of my grandmother. I remember the cards she sent to people who were scared and hurting. I remember her phone calls to the sick. I remember the check she wrote to her church faithfully, even when she barely had enough to get by, and the joy on the faces of the people who graciously received her gifts.

Because I have accepted those gracious gifts, I am able to see a ray of light at the end of a long, dark tunnel. The Bible says in the book of Revelation, "Whoever is thirsty, let him come; and whoever wishes, let him take the free gift of the water of life" (22:17) I thank God for His promises. I thank God for the gifts from those precious people. And today, I thank my grandmother for a lesson finally learned.

Without real focus, it's hard to build a strong foundation

The little storage building was in bad need of repair. It had been in the backyard of my parents' house for years and had weathered many years of packing and stacking. From old glass jars and cardboard boxes, the building served not only as a catch-all for clutter but also provided a safe place for things that my mother wanted to keep but no longer could find room for in the house. She called it "her" building and cherished the space that she could call her own.

But Mama's safe place was becoming an eyesore. The wood was rotting and the roof leaked. She began moving her things out so they wouldn't be ruined. My mother had almost decided to get rid of the building altogether when my brother assured her that her building could be fixed.

He had done a lot of work and bought a truck full of supplies when he called in the troops. I've never been much of a carpenter, but I hoped that I would be able to help. Before I knew it, I had a hammer in my hand and instructions to go with it.

"You see these rusty nails everywhere? Pull them out. Start on the outside. I want to get the siding up tonight, and we have to get rid of all these nails first."

I grabbed a hammer and began to work. It took a little effort, but soon I caught on. Hook, yank, drop it in the bucket. I was getting pretty good at this. Before I knew it, that job was finished. I was beginning to feel like a real carpenter.

"What's next?" I asked, pausing to look at the sky. A storm was brewing, and we needed to hurry.

"Siding," he said. "We need to get it up before the storm comes." This was not a job that I could handle by myself, but my husband quickly came to my rescue.

"Here," my brother instructed, "hold it straight and then use this electric staple gun to hold it in place. Then use these nails and hammer them in here and here," he said, pointing.

Easy enough. I had my instructions. Place, hold, staple. I picked up a few nails and my hammer. It was time to drive those nails in and finish up this piece of siding. *Tap, tap, tap,* I began. Not hard enough. *Tap, ping!* The nail flew out into the grass beside the building. I picked up the nail and tried again. It bounced on the ground again. I glanced over to see my husband's perfect row of nails. It didn't look as hard as I was making it.

Well, I'll get it this time, I thought.

Whack! I smashed my thumb with the hammer. I looked at the darkening sky.

I needed to hurry. *Tap, ping! Whack!*

What is wrong with me? I groaned to myself. My husband noticed my trouble and tried to help, but I shooed him away like a stubborn child. "It's *my* nail," I said. "Let me do it myself."

By the time the storm hit, my thumb was throbbing, and we weren't nearly finished with our job. I dashed inside my mother's house and thought about my dilemma. I knew what was wrong, and I finally admitted it to myself. I was afraid. Not only was I afraid to hold onto the nail after I smashed my thumb the first time, but I was afraid to look.

Rather than focusing on the nail, I was focused on the storm. I was focused on my son and my six-year-old nephew, stewing over how easy even they made it look to hammer a nail. I was in a hurry. I was stubborn and wanted to do it all by myself, embarrassed that I couldn't even hit the nail on the head and drive it in.

The few times I did drive the nail through the siding, I realized that I had missed the stud that I should have nailed it to. If it hadn't been for my husband's nails anchoring the siding to the frame, it would have been on the ground like my nails.

How many times have I encountered the same problem in my Christian life? Always in a hurry. Focusing on the storms in my life rather than focusing on the One who can calm the storms. Too embarrassed to ask for help when I needed it or instructions when I didn't know how. Not learning the lesson the first time and hurting myself the same way over and over. Thinking that I am accomplishing something, only to find my hard work dashed to the ground because there was no anchor, no foundation.

Focus. Whether it is in my Christian life or in my life as an amateur carpenter, I am sure to fail if I lose focus on what is most important. The Bible says in Hebrews 12:2, "Let us fix our eyes on Jesus, the author and perfecter of our faith . . . "

Before long, the storm had ended, and I returned to my work. *Focus*, I reminded myself. And, you guessed it, the more I focused, the better I got. Soon I was able to stand back and admire my handiwork.

Wouldn't it be wonderful to live a life so fixed on the author and perfecter of our faith that He would some day look on us, His handiwork, with admiration? I don't know about you, but a "well done" from the Savior would be plenty enough for me.

They grow up much too quickly

I saw the sparkle in her eyes before I saw the glittering ring on her finger. With the family gathered at my husband's parents' house on Christmas Day, our sweet young niece was glowing, anxious to show off the beautiful diamond ring that her boyfriend had given her on Christmas Eve.

As I rushed over to hug her and admire her ring, I caught a glimpse of her mother out of the corner of my eye.

"Have you set a date?" I asked my niece.

"Not yet," she answered.

"She's too young to get married," I heard her mother mutter. "She's just a baby, my baby girl."

Her "baby girl" had just graduated from college. She will be twenty-two years old in April. I could tell that my sister-in-law was teasing her daughter, but at the same time, she meant what she said.

"Let's see," I asked my sister-in-law slyly, "how old were you when you got married?"

"I was twenty-two," she replied. "But I was an old twenty-two."

Me too. I had been twenty-two for three whole weeks, in fact, when I said my "I do's." I was ready to tease my sister-in-law again when I glanced over at my own twenty-one-year-old son, only four months younger than his cousin. I quickly clamped my hand over my mouth.

Where have the years gone? It seems like yesterday that all the little cousins were underfoot, having their "Cousin Kangaroo" meetings at our house, baking cookies, and riding a big blow-up dinosaur around the den.

I had made them matching kangaroo shirts and video-taped them singing songs they learned in Bible school. I painted the girls' faces as the boys climbed trees and played in the sandpile.

And now? Besides the engaged one, another is grown and has a job working with children. One is a preacher in Pennsylvania. One is applying to medical school. One is in college studying to be an engineer. The youngest cousin has only one year left in high school after this semester.

And their mothers? We're quickly closing in on thirty-year high school reunions. Who would have ever thought the time could have passed so quickly?

Just the other day, I ran into an old high school friend at the store.

"How old are your children now?" she had asked.

"About our age," I answered. I could tell that she knew exactly what I meant, but I began to explain anyway. "You know, the age we were not so long ago. The age we're supposed to be."

"I know..." she replied, her voice trailing off. Maybe her mind had wandered to the Philippines where her oldest son had just spent Christmas with the Peace Corps.

I know, I know. What else could I possibly want for these children? They have all been raised in good homes. They have been loved and supported by Christian parents and grandparents. They have been disciplined and trained. They have been held through the hard times.

They have made wise choices, for the most part, and have learned from their mistakes. They have grown in their love for their families and for each other and in their love for the Lord. They are kind and compassionate, and some day, they will make wonderful parents themselves.

But for some reason, it's still hard to watch them grow and go. The Bible says, in Ecclesiastes 3:1, "There is a time for everything and a season for every activity under heaven." Yes, a season for our babies to grow up, leave home, and even get married.

So to my beautiful young niece, I will give the same advice that I have given to my own sons: "Trust in the Lord with all your heart and lean not to your own understanding. In all your ways acknowledge Him, and He will direct your paths" (Proverbs 3:5–6).

Just the other day, I found a Cousin Kangaroo plate that I had made for the cousins many years ago. I know it was silly, but I picked up that old plate and hugged it to my heart and kissed it before I put it back in the cabinet. Ah, precious memories.

No matter how much they grow or how far they go, the Cousin Kangaroos will always have a special place in my heart and in my prayers.

Wedding dress serves as a reminder of gifts made with love

"Guess what I did while you boys and Dad were out washing cars this afternoon?" I answered my own question before my son could speak. I knew that he would never guess, anyway. "I tried on my wedding dress."

My twenty-year-old son looked at me curiously. Mothers of grown sons who have been married for nearly twenty-seven years just don't try their wedding gowns on every day. The truth is, it was the first time that I had put the dress on since I had worn it on a special summer day way back in 1979.

"Why?" he couldn't help but ask. He already suspected that I had more to say.

He was right. There were actually lots of reasons. Earlier

that day, my husband and I had attended the fiftieth wedding anniversary party of the parents of my best friend in high school. I had not seen my friend in years, and the afternoon had brought back a flood of wonderful memories.

Maybe it was the fifty years of marriage that we were celebrating that led me to the top corner of my closet and the brown box that had remained untouched for years. Perhaps it was the picture of my friend's daughter wearing her mother's wedding dress in her own wedding just a few months earlier. As I looked at the young bride in her mother's wedding gown, it occurred to me, as the mother of sons, that the dress that I had packed away so carefully would probably never be worn again. The least I could do was try it on one more time.

It's still white, I thought as I carefully pulled away the paper that had cradled the dress for years. As I slipped into my wedding dress, I thought of the story behind my dress. There is always a story, you know.

My friend's mother was a wonderful seamstress and had made most of her daughter's clothes when we were in school together. When my friend decided to get married, her mother had tackled the most important sewing job of her life. She had made my friend's wedding dress. She had done a beautiful job. But that's not all—as a gift to me a few years later, she also offered to make my wedding dress.

She had helped me pick a pattern and the right material for the dress. We had shopped for lace and buttons. And now, decades later, as I stood in front of the mirror in the gown made by my friend's mother, I knew that every stitch in that dress was a labor of love.

How do you thank someone for a gift like that? As I

hugged my friend's mother good-bye and once again congratulated her on fifty years of marriage, we finally talked about the dress.

"Could you send me a picture of your wedding dress?" she asked. "I want to show Cheryl," she said. "Can you believe that she didn't even remember that I made your dress?"

What? How could she not remember something that important? She had been my best friend. But then I realized something. The gift had not been hers. It was mine. It was important to me in a way that she could never know. I had accepted the gift, and it had made a difference in my life. Every time I had thought of my wedding through the years, every time I had looked at my wedding album, I had thought about the special lady who had offered me a free gift, just for the taking.

I have been offered another gift too, just for the taking. And I have accepted that gift. I did nothing to earn it and surely didn't deserve it.

The Bible talks over and over about the gift of salvation. Through the years, every time I think of that gift, I think of the One who gave it to me. I think of the difference it has made in my life. I think about the happy times, times when I raised my hands in praise to the Lord. Then I think about the hard times, times when His strength and comfort sustained me until I could hope again. And every time and in every circumstance, I thank Him for the gift that changed my life.

"So, what do you think?" I asked my son as I held up the dress for him to see for the first time. He just nodded his head. I could tell that it was just an old-fashioned dress to him, nothing special at all. He couldn't possibly know what it meant to me. But that's okay, because it was my gift, made with love, and made especially for me.

The wisdom of age
is not always lost on the young

"I saw two people that I haven't seen in a while today," I announced to my youngest son when I returned from a late-evening meeting. "Both of them told me that they were praying for you. So two more people have added you to their prayer lists."

It was my son's first day of college. After a challenging year, he finally felt it was time to take a few classes and get back to some semblance of the "real" life of an eighteen-year-old. He was a little apprehensive, but the day seemed to have gone well. It was the first time we had a chance to talk about his day.

"Make that three," he answered. I looked at him curiously. "Well, I met someone today."

A friend? Already? Many of my son's friends had chosen to go away to college, and he, in more ways than one, had been left behind. But now he was telling me that he had met someone who had already pledged to pray for him. I had prayed for him to find a Christian friend who would have a firm, godly influence in his life. Could this be the answer to my prayers?

"Well, I met him in the Cube," he explained. "The line was so long in the bookstore that they told us to wait there." He went on to say that he had been sitting at a table with some boys he knew from high school until they had to leave for class. This is when this new person approached him.

"He had signed up to take a class. He'd had a hard year, and he felt that he needed to do something, to get out of the house."

Like you, I thought.

"So he decided to take a computer course."

This is good, I mused. *Come on, come on,* I silently pleaded. *Get to the part where he said that he would pray for you.*

"You see, Mom, his wife died a month ago."

"His wife?"

My son continued without skipping a beat. "Yes, his wife. She's the one who knew all about the computer. So when she died, he was lonely, and he missed being able to get the news and the weather on the computer. He liked using e-mail too. But he didn't know how to use it without her help. So he signed up for the computer class."

The news and the weather?

"How old is this person?" I finally asked.

"Oh, he's eighty-one. Did I tell you that his wife died? And that he had done mission work in Africa? He was held at gunpoint one time, he told me. Oh, and, Mom, he helped rebuild a church in a valley. They were going to make the church into a water plant, so they had to move it. They're getting ready to have the fiftieth anniversary of their church in a few weeks, and he sure does hope that he lives long enough to go to the celebration."

The young eighteen-year-old buddy that I had imagined for my son was quickly fading, shrinking into a stooped, white-haired old gentleman. *A mere reversal of numbers,* I thought to myself. *Not 18, but 81, the difference of a whole lifetime.*

My son had spent the first semester of school this year alternating his days between his grandparents' houses. Because of health reasons, we thought this would be best for him. I had noticed a change in his attitude, a real difference in him as he kept my mother company and helped her with my daddy, who has Alzheimer's disease. He had accompanied my mother to her exercise classes at the hospital and had told me of many conversations that he had with the senior citizens in that program.

He had spent a lot of time with his other grandparents too. They had taken him places and told him things about our family that he didn't know. He had changed the brake pads on his car with the help of his granddaddy.

I had told him over and over that although it may not seem like it now, when he wanted to be living the normal life of an eighteen-year-old, that the time he had been able to spend with his grandparents would be a blessing that he would cherish his whole life.

"Boys your age are too busy to do what you are doing," I told him. *"You have been given this treasured time that few are able to enjoy."*

My son had shared with the elderly gentleman a little about his own struggles. And his new friend had promised to pray for him as he began college. It reminded me of the lady at the Christian Women's Club who told me recently that every morning at 6:30 she prays for my son. Every morning she calls his name out to our Heavenly Father, beseeching His blessings on behalf of my precious boy.

In a society where the aged are often ignored or mistreated, we would do well to remember the words of Leviticus 19:32, "Rise in the presence of the aged, show respect for the elderly." For with age comes wisdom and understanding. With age comes an extra prayer for an eighteen-year-old boy from an eighty-one-year-old friend.

Oh, that I should be so faithful. Thank you, Lord, for sending my son a new friend. You never cease to amaze me.

Time has come to let him go

"Go ahead and open it," my oldest son said. "I know what it's going to say, but you can read it to me anyway."

I was expecting him to come home that day for the Christmas holidays. I knew he had finished up at work the day before. I was using the letter as an excuse to call the boy who still doesn't like to be "checked up on" to find out when he was coming home.

We had been through this scenario before. It was just a little letter. We both knew all about little letters. Little letters had cordial greetings but the same old standard message. Sometimes the words were different, but the message was always the same.

"Thanks, but no thanks. We appreciate your time and

interest. You are an excellent candidate, but not suited to our institution. You have been placed on a waiting list ... "

That's what we both had expected this time too, but at least it was a reason for me to call this oldest son and a reason for him to listen.

The letter was from a medical school where he had interviewed the week before. He had been relentless in his efforts throughout the summer and fall as he wrote essays and filled out applications. In the past month, he had interviewed at four medical schools with several more interviews scheduled after the holidays.

"Where are you, by the way?" I asked as I peeled at the flap of the envelope.

"Oh, I'm still in Chapel Hill," he explained. "I'm volunteering for hospice this afternoon." He went on to say that the patient was an elderly lady with Alzheimer's disease. The nurse had to run some errands, so my son was alone with the lady.

"I'm not bothering you, am I?" I asked. "If you're busy, I can talk to you later," I said.

"No, it's okay. She's asleep. I was reading a book. You can talk." By that time, I had slipped the little letter out of the little envelope.

"Dear Mr. Smith," I read out loud, "I am truly delighted to offer you a place in the 2006 entering class ... "

I heard a funny sound on the other end of the phone and a click as my husband grabbed up the cordless phone in the kitchen.

"Mama, you're not playing a trick on me, are you? Mama, are you sure you're reading that little letter right?"

With his dad looking over my shoulder, he assured him that Mama was indeed reading the little letter right.

"Shhh..." I quieted him, "don't wake the lady. I'm telling the truth. Now, would you like me to read the rest of the letter to you?"

I read the letter nice and slowly as my son soaked in every word. I had his complete attention as I continued.

"It is with respect for your past accomplishments and anticipation of your contributions... that this offer of acceptance is advanced."

"I'm coming home," he said. "I want to read that letter for myself."

"Don't you leave the lady until the nurse gets back," I heard myself saying to my seven-year-old son in his twenty-two-year-old body.

"Mama," he groaned. The boy had just been accepted into medical school, and I was still talking to him in my *mama* voice. I was going to have to work on that.

As I fingered the little letter over and over, reading and rereading the words, I thought of the enormity of the message. For my son, it meant that years of hard work and perseverance had finally paid off. It meant that he could move on with his life, working toward the goal that he had set years ago. For me, it meant that once again my faith would be tested. I have asked the Lord to use him. I have asked Him to be my son's protector when that is no longer required of me. Now it is my job to trust. It is my job to support and to love, and, yes, sometimes to mind my own business, as the Lord directs my son.

There is another little letter that I have read recently

that has spoken volumes to me. It is the letter in the Bible that Paul wrote to a man named Philemon. In his letter, he appeals in love to Philemon on behalf of a Christian brother named Onesimus. He refers to Onesimus as his son, his spiritual son, his true son in the faith. "I am sending him—who is my very heart—back to you. I would have liked to keep him with me" (Philemon 12–13).

I would have liked to keep my son with me too. But the message is loud and clear, despite the size of the letter. It is time. So, Lord, today I am sending my son, who is my very heart, back to you. Use him, guide him, protect him. And always remind him, Lord, that little is much when You are in it.

Daddy's lessons about life stay with me even now

"How would you rank yourself in your ability to communicate with the staff if you were to become the lead teacher?"

I took a deep breath. I could imagine my daddy sitting beside me, his hand resting on my shoulder, nodding for me to answer the question.

It had been a long time since I had sat in this seat. I had been teaching in a reading intervention class for eight years. I loved my job and enjoyed working with the students. I guess I should have realized that my dream job would not last forever.

So I was interviewing for a new job. I had read over the job description and had prepared for the interview, but as

I walked into the room with middle school principals and county office personnel, I could feel the butterflies in the pit of my stomach.

"We're going to ask you ten questions," one of the principals explained. "You have thirty minutes to answer the questions, so pace yourself." Again, I looked over at my daddy. Well, not really. But as sure as I ever felt anything, I felt his support. I felt him urging me on, heard his voice in my head. I was twelve years old again and looking for the nod of approval from the daddy whom I adored.

My daddy had been a teacher too. He was my first role model, my mentor. He had been so proud when I had decided to become a teacher.

"It's the perfect job for a mother," he would say. "You'll have the same hours as your children, the same holidays." He could go on and on about the advantages of being a teacher. But more than his words, I could tell by his actions. Whether it was coaching football, teaching history or driver education, I never heard him complain about the long hours he put into his job. When he heard about a student who was a discipline problem, the first day the child walked into Daddy's class, he made sure that he sent him on an errand. Daddy often told me that he held his breath, knowing that he probably shouldn't trust the child but praying that he could.

"Sometimes that's all it takes," Daddy explained. "They need to know that somebody is willing to take a chance on them." Daddy was willing.

"My daddy told me never to toot my own horn," I finally answered. I went on to explain the lessons that I had learned from him. How it's not just what you say, but how you say it. I talked about being a good listener and an encourager.

The following Sunday, our family gathered at my sister's house for lunch. My brothers and their families were there too. One brother, the assistant superintendent of another school system, asked me how my interview went.

I looked over at my daddy. All these years and I had never noticed how blue his eyes were. I held his hand as I talked, smiling and nodding. I wanted him to know how much I loved and respected him. I wanted him to know how much he had taught me, how thankful I was that God had loved me enough to choose him to be my father.

But I wasn't even sure he knew who I was. I hadn't heard him call me by name in a long time. He seemed to be in a fairly good mood, but I knew that could change at any minute. It had only been weeks before that he sat at the dining room table at his home, crying about all the strangers in his house. The family had met for lunch at my parents' house on Sundays after church for years. But the confusion, the Alzheimer's, the doctors called it, was especially bad that day. So everyone had cleared out of the dining room except me.

"I don't know why I'm crying," Daddy said.

"It's okay, Daddy," I said. "Let's sing."

Daddy began to sing every word of the old hymns that he had loved all his life.

"Just a little talk with Jesus makes it right," his rich bass voice boomed.

My daddy wasn't a big talker when it came to spiritual matters, but he had always witnessed to me in perfect harmony when we sang together.

"What a day that will be when my Savior I shall see" and "When they ring those golden bells for you and me," we sang. By the time we finished, tears were rolling down my cheeks too.

"See, Daddy, I don't know why I'm crying either," I said as we just enjoyed the moment together.

I hope I told my daddy how much I loved him when he could understand. I hope I told him how much I appreciated his loving lessons in my life. But for now, it is enough to hold his hand, enough to be in his presence, enough to be his daughter. For that, I will be forever grateful.

By the way, I got the job. For a moment I can imagine that my daddy understands, that he is sitting beside me, his hand resting on my shoulder, nodding his approval.

Thank you, Daddy. You taught me well.

Safe return of son provides a reason to give thanks

December 21, my mother's birthday, and I am in the airport looking for familiar shoes. My husband and I have scoped the terminal and found the right gate, we are sure. We have checked the arrival board to make sure that the plane has arrived and now wait anxiously as feet and legs slowly transform into whole bodies as they make their way down the escalator toward their loved ones.

We had not seen our oldest son in months. His brother had dropped him off at this same airport early one the morning to go live in another country with another family. But today he was coming home. He would spend two weeks at home for the Christmas holidays. I couldn't wait.

Neither could his dad.

"Come on," he said, grabbing my hand. "We don't have to wait down here. Let's go up those stairs and wait at the top."

Finally, I saw that familiar face. I wrapped my arms around him. He had traveled 2,455 miles from Quito, Ecuador, to Charlotte, North Carolina, not to mention a nine-hour bus trip to get from his home in Portoviejo to the airport in Quito. I looked at my watch. Four twenty-seven. His plane had been scheduled to arrive at four thirty.

I thanked the Lord for His faithfulness to our family and His answers to my prayers. People stranded in airports everywhere and my boy was right here, right on time. "I will lift up my eyes to the hills—where does my help come from? My help comes from the Lord, the Maker of heaven and earth" (Psalm 121:1–2).

The ride home from the airport could have been long and miserable. The traffic was terrible. But I hardly noticed. Our son began to tell us stories of his life in Portoviejo. He told about his classes at the university where he teaches and about his students. I thought he might tell us about his students' progress in learning to speak English. But instead he told us of playing bingo with them and tossing them a piece of candy as a prize when they won.

"They can't catch, Mama," he said. "They don't teach their children to throw and catch a ball like we do in America. It's not a 'throw and catch' culture. When I throw a ball to Joselito (his two-year-old host brother), if he does happen to catch it, he drops it and kicks it. I guess he'll be a soccer player like everyone else."

I read later that it is actually rude to toss things to people, like candy or keys. They accept it from a "gringo," an American who doesn't know any better, but would never let a Latin American get by with such bad manners.

When we got home, he downloaded hundreds of pictures for us to see. One day I clicked on a video clip, thinking it was just another digital picture. All of the sudden, the hilly landscape was whizzing by and I realized that my boy was in the open bed of a truck, speeding around curving dirt roads, being driven by one of those "crazy" drivers that he had described to us.

When I caught my breath, I again thanked God for his faithfulness to our family. "He will not let your foot slip—he who watches over you will not slumber; indeed he who watches over Israel (and Ecuador) will neither slumber nor sleep" (Psalm 121:3–4).

On Christmas morning my husband laughed as my son picked up one of the gifts that I had given him.

"I wonder when you'll wear this UNC toboggan in Ecuador."

Ecuador is named because of its location on the equator. The altitude is so high in Quito, my son explained, that you can get sunburned in seventy-degree weather. Their hot season, out on the coast where he lives, is January through March, so he hasn't experienced the real heat yet.

"I have a fan," he said. "No, Mom, I don't think I'll be needing the toboggan for a while."

"The Lord watches over you—the Lord is your shade at your right hand; the sun will not harm you by day, nor the moon by night" (Psalm 121:5–6).

The days have passed so quickly. My oldest boy has eaten

chicken and ham instead of cow udders and guinea pig. He has spent time with his brothers and visited with friends and family. But in a few short days it is back to the airport and a ride up the escalator this time. He will be gone until the end of July. Some days I don't know if I can make it, but this I know for sure, and I claim this promise for all of my sons today.

"The Lord will keep you from all harm—He will watch over your life; the Lord will watch over your coming and going both now and forevermore" (Psalm 121:7–8).

Amen.

Son reminds mother of lessons learned

"Mom, I'm home."

I looked out the window. "No, you're not," I said. "I don't see you anywhere."

The voice on the phone wasn't the sing-songy *"I'm ho-ome"* that I would have expected from a boy who had stolen away from college for a quick visit home for the night.

"You're right. I am in Lexington. But Mom..."

I could hear the stress, feel the tension through the phone lines. I waited for him to continue. A mechanical engineering major, this boy had already shared with me his woes over his difficult engineering classes. Last semester it was the professor with an accent so thick that my son couldn't understand what he was saying. Then it was the lost project grade when the lines of communication had somehow crossed between a teaching assistant and a professor. He was so thankful when that had finally been resolved. He had made it through that semester, but this semester, he wasn't so sure.

As I listened to my son, it was like hearing his dad speak thirty years ago. My husband had majored in electrical engineering. Over the years our son has watched his dad become a successful engineer who enjoys his job. But I remembered hearing the same frustrations and the same doubts from his dad as he also struggled to stand under an insurmountable load of work as a young man pursuing a degree in engineering.

"Mom, I just can't do it," he went on. It had been a while since he had been home; too much work, too little time. But he had thought that he had worked it out for this one night. That is, until he had checked his e-mail when he got to his girlfriend's house.

"I knew that my meeting was tomorrow at one o'clock. But I just found out that my group wants me to bring my part of the presentation to the meeting. It's our junior engineering project, Mom. I haven't even started on it. I haven't had time. There's no way I can spend the night at home and get all that work done." So I did what any good mother would do. I gave him advice.

"Listen," I said, "go get something to eat and relax for a few minutes." I told him to spend some time with his girlfriend, a sweet girl who is a good listener. "Don't worry about coming by home. Just go on back to school and give yourself enough time to work so you won't be so stressed."

"Thank you, Mama," I heard him say quietly. "You're a good mama."

"Besides," I continued, "if you don't finish, there is probably someone in your group who will help you when you get to your meeting."

"No, Mama. I don't want to be one of those kids."

I smiled. I knew exactly what he meant. As a teacher, I've seen it over and over: one student doing all the work while the others sit back and do nothing, a few carrying the weight of many. I was glad that my son wanted to pull his own weight, even in the times when the weight was almost more than he could bear.

I never wanted to be one of those students either. And as an adult, there are other things that I don't want to be. I don't want to be the one who speaks before I think. I don't want to be a person who jumps to conclusions and carelessly throws around words that hurt people. I don't want to wear a sour face, always looking at the empty glass, making people turn the other way when they see me coming.

I don't want to be crude or rude or hateful. I don't want to feel sorry for myself, wallowing in my own self-pity. I don't want to huddle with the complainers when things don't go my way. I don't want to be part of the problem. I want to be part of the solution.

For it is then, and only then, that I can call myself a follower of Christ. Oh, I might believe in Him, and I might claim to be a Christian. But I am certainly not following Him if my attitude is not like that of Jesus. Paul, in his letter to the Philippians, tells us exactly what the Lord expects of us who call ourselves Christians.

"Whatever is honorable, whatever is just, whatever is pure, whatever is pleasing, whatever is commendable, if there is any excellence and if there is anything worthy of praise, think about these things" (Philippians 4:8).

For as a man thinketh, so is he.

Think about excellence, and you will be excellent. That's about the best advice that I can give to my son these days. And sometimes it takes a son to remind a mother of the best lessons of all.

Life with three sons turned out to be just fine

"It's a boy. Another boy."

The doctor spoke confidently. I remember his expression, his tone of voice, like it was yesterday instead of nearly eighteen years ago.

"In fact," he added, "I'm so sure that if it's a girl, I'll give you one hundred dollars to start her a savings account."

I remember walking across the parking lot after my appointment and groaning to my husband. "I feel like I'm going to live in a smelly old locker room for the rest of my life."

It wasn't that I didn't love the two boys that we already had. I knew I'd love that third boy too. But for months I'd had a tiny glimmer of hope that someday soon I would have my little girl. My doctor had even worn a pink tie and pink socks for one of my appointments. But he was also quick to remind me that he was a third son himself, and he had turned out just fine.

And life with three sons has turned out just fine. Given the choice, I would choose my sons over and over again, for they are my joy every day. They are precious gifts of God, and we are blessed because of them. But it has not been easy. For a little girl like me, who never even had dirt under her fingernails, raising boys has been a challenge. When I was a child, my idea of fun was to read a good book and snuggle with my puppy. It never crossed my mind to roam the woods with a rusty machete, jump ramps on a dirt bike, or throw water balloons at cars.

I was clean. My boys have been dirty. I walked, and they ran. I was quiet, and they have been loud. I was safe, and they have been reckless.

We used to go to the park so they could play on the playground equipment while I walked on the walking trail.

"No stacking," I'd say. But no sooner than I could get it out of my mouth, they'd be lying on top of each other, speeding down the slide headfirst.

"No jumping," I continued. But as they pushed each other higher and higher on the swings, it wasn't long before one was sailing through the air and tumbling on the ground in a fit of laughter.

It wasn't that I was trying to stop their fun. I was trying to be a good mother. I was trying to raise safe, responsible boys.

And then there was the merry-go-round. As a child, it was my favorite. On the old wooden platform, I found my special spot, right in the middle. Sometimes I would stand. Other times, I would lie on my back and look up at the clouds. I enjoyed the gentle twirling. It was always someone else, a brother, perhaps, running alongside, making the merry-go-round spin. I could hear the laughter and screams of the other children, children who dared go to the outer edge where they had to hold on for dear life. But not me. I liked the safety of the center.

I still do. But the screams and the laughter of the world have beckoned my sons to the edge. For the most part, they have been able to hang on to the bars. Even when they have stumbled a bit, most of the time they have been able to pick themselves up, brush off, and rejoin the fun. But sometimes they have fallen hard. There have been bumps and bruises along the way, even some scars to remind them when they have strayed too close to the edge and have been hurled to the ground.

My boys are young men now. They are making major life decisions in a world that often seems, like the merry-go-round, to be spinning out of control. I will continue to remind them that there is safety in the center, but only if they make Jesus, and only Jesus, the center of their lives. They can't make their careers the center. They can't even make family relationships the center of their lives. For if they do, they will never experience the peace that God has to offer them.

I will tell them that if they keep Jesus Lord of their lives, "a thousand may fall at your side, ten thousand at your right hand, but it (deadly pestilence) will not come near you" (Psalms 91:7). I will remind them that "if you will make the

Most High your dwelling—even the Lord who is my refuge, then no harm will befall you" (Psalms 91:9–10). And I will remind myself that sometimes all I can do for my boys is to obey God when he tells me to be still and wait patiently as He works in their lives.

Yes, some days I do smell the stench of the locker room. Other days I am surrounded with a fragrance too wonderful to describe. After all these years I realize, with the Lord's help, even smelly boys can be a breath of fresh air.

The desires of a mother's heart for her children

"Mama, someday I'm going to write a song about you, about how you're such a good mama and about how much you help me."

I smiled and patted my middle son on the knee. I hoped he could tell by the bobbing of my head that I thought that was a sweet thing to say. I was too tired to answer.

I had spent the whole weekend being a good mama, catering to the needs of each son. The youngest one had needed a ride to the mall. After a half-hour conversation on the way home about why in the world he would want to pay sixteen dollars for a three-dollar T-shirt, I was pretty worn out.

Then the oldest one surprised me when he stopped by home for a few hours on his way to visit a friend. We had forgotten to take a trash can for his room at college, so I made a mad dash to the store so he would have one to take back with him. I bought it this time, but, of course, he forgot to take it with him.

Then there was the songwriter. He's a college boy himself and loaded down with work. It was Sunday afternoon by this time.

"Not much weekend left," I was muttering to myself when I heard him call for me.

"Mama, I really need help on this assignment. I'm not sure what my teacher wants. Could you help me?"

I glanced at the dirty dishes in the sink and the pile of clothes that needed to be folded.

"Sure I can," I told him. "I'll be glad to." So we pulled out his books. I read and explained. He listened and asked questions. We researched together, taking turns discussing the project. We had plowed through about half of the assignment when I looked at the clock.

"Oops," I said. "It's almost church time again. I have to play the piano and pick up your brother. He should be back from the youth trip by the time church is over. Maybe I can help you again when I get home."

And maybe he'll be finished and I can do some work of my own, I thought to myself.

But he wasn't. After working about an hour after I got home from church, I finally thought he could handle the assignment alone. I went downstairs to read my devotions when I looked up to see him standing in the kitchen.

"Mom, I really need to study chemistry. I thought maybe we could double team this stuff. You work on the project, and I'll study."

It was eleven thirty-one the next time I looked at the clock. The boy was mumbling something about "Good Mama" and writing a song. I stumbled to bed.

Six o'clock came early the next morning. As I opened my sleepy eyes, I remembered what my son had said to me the night before. Then I thought about all the years of love and devotion and sweat and tears that I have put into raising these boys. And I thought about what I really want.

Boys, I want you to love God with all your hearts, all your souls, and all your minds. I want you to go to church faithfully and devote yourselves to the work of the Lord, serving God and serving others with compassionate hearts. I want you to honor and respect your parents and grandparents and live long, happy lives. I want you to devote yourselves to your brothers, always being faithful to the family with which God has blessed you. I want you to study God's Word and pray without ceasing. I want you to be godly men and raise godly families. And always, I want Jesus to be your strength and your comfort and the sweet, sweet love of your souls.

And then yes, my middle son, you can write that song about your mama. But if there is any praise, let it be to the One who fills your mama's heart with love, the One who holds your mama close to His own heart, and, most of all, to the One who loved your mama enough to bless her with three precious sons.

That's right. Sing to the Lord a new song, my son. A song of praise, hallelujah!

About the Author

Donna Tobin Smith is a wife and mother of three sons, ages 24, 22, and 20. She is the lead teacher at Central Davidson Middle School in Lexington, North Carolina. A graduate of the University of North Carolina at Charlotte with a master's degree in Human Development and Learning, she spent her sons' young years as a stay-at-home mom before returning to teaching in an outreach program targeting struggling learners. She is a dedicated member of her church, Bethel United Methodist Church in Thomasville, where she serves as Sunday school teacher of an adult class and pianist.

As past chairman and prayer advisor of Stonecroft Ministries Lexington chapter of Christian Women's Club, Donna enjoys speaking for various women's groups in her area. Since 1996 she has written a monthly religion column in *The Dispatch*, Lexington's hometown newspaper. She would love to hear from you. You may contact her at muddyfeet519@yahoo.com.